WITH... ...FROM
TH...
UNIVERSITY OF

KT-466-067

DAVID EDGAR

David Edgar took up playwriting after a short career in journalism.

His original plays for the theatre include *Death Story* for the Birmingham Repertory Theatre, *Saigon Rose* for the Traverse Theatre in Edinburgh, *Wreckers* for 7:84 England, *That Summer* for Hampstead Theatre and *Entertaining Strangers*, first as a community play for Dorchester and then at the National Theatre. His original plays for the RSC include *Destiny, Maydays* and *Pentecost* (winner of the Evening Standard Best Play Award in 1995). *Pentecost* was the second of a series of plays about Eastern Europe after the Cold War, following *The Shape of the Table* (NT) and preceding *The Prisoner's Dilemma* (RSC). *Continental Divide*, his two-play cycle about American politics, comprising the plays *Mothers Against* and *Daughters of the Revolution*, was premiered at the Oregon Shakespeare Festival and Berkeley Rep, before transferring to the Birmingham Repertory Theatre and the Barbican Centre in London.

His adaptations include *Mary Barnes* for the Birmingham Repertory Theatre; *The Jail Diary of Albie Sachs*, a Tony Award-winning adaptation of Dickens' *Nicholas Nickleby* and a new dramatisation of Stevenson's *Dr Jekyll and Mr Hyde* for the RSC; and a play based on Gitta Sereny's biography of Albert Speer for the National Theatre.

David Edgar has also written for television and radio, and wrote the screenplay for Trevor Nunn's film *Lady Jane*. He founded and directed Britain's first postgraduate course in playwriting at the University of Birmingham from 1989 to 1999; he was appointed professor in 1995.

KA 0295073 1

Other Titles in this Series

David Edgar

PLAYING
WITH FIRE

NICK HERN BOOKS
London
www.nickhernbooks.co.uk

A Nick Hern Book

Playing with Fire first published in Great Britain
as a paperback original in 2005 by Nick Hern Books Limited,
14 Larden Road, London W3 7ST

Playing with Fire copyright © 2005 David Edgar
Afterword copyright © 2005 David Edgar

Cover image: © EMPICS

David Edgar has asserted his right to be identified as
the author of this work

Typeset by Country Setting, Kingsdown, Kent CT14 8ES
Printed in Great Britain by Bookmarque, Croydon, Surrey

A CIP catalogue record for this book is available from
the British Library

ISBN-13   978 1 85459 880 6
ISBN-10   1 85459 880 5

CAUTION   All rights whatsoever in this play are strictly reserved.
Requests to reproduce the text in whole or in part should be
addressed to the publisher.

Amateur Performing Rights   Applications for performance,
including readings and excerpts, by amateurs should be
addressed to the Performing Rights Manager, Nick Hern Books,
14 Larden Road, London W3 7ST, *fax* +44 (0)20 8735 0250,
e-mail info@nickhernbooks.demon.co.uk, except as follows:

Australia: Dominie Drama, 8 Cross Street, Brookvale 2100,
fax (2) 9905 5209, *e-mail* dominie@dominie.com.au

New Zealand: Play Bureau, PO Box 420, New Plymouth,
fax (6)753 2150, *e-mail* play.bureau.nz@xtra.co.nz

United States of Canada and Canada: Alan Brodie Representation,
see details below

Professional Performing Rights   Applications for performance by
professionals in any medium and in any language throughout the
world should be addressed to Alan Brodie Representation Ltd, 6th
Floor, Fairgate House, 78 New Oxford Street, London WC1A 1HB,
fax +44 (0)20 7079 7999, *e-mail* info@alanbrodie.com

No performance of any kind may be given unless a licence has
been obtained. Applications should be made before rehearsals
begin. Publication of this play does not necessarily indicate its
availability for performance.

To Sue Clegg and Derek Howl

Playing with Fire was first performed in the Olivier auditorium of the National Theatre, London, on 21 September 2005 (previews from 12 September). The cast was as follows:

LONDON

Alex Clifton, *a civil servant*	Emma Fielding
Stephen Croft, *a minister*	Alistair Petrie
Joe McIntyre, *an assistant*	Colin Haigh
Leena Harvey Wells, *a consultant*	Sameena Zehra

THE COUNCIL

George Aldred, *Leader of Wyverdale Council*	David Troughton
Jack Ross, *Labour councillor*	Ewan Stewart
Anwar Hafiz, *Labour councillor*	Aaron Neil
Arthur Barraclough, *Labour councillor*	Trevor Cooper
Frank Wilkins, *Labour councillor*	Oliver Ford Davies
Maureen Teale, *The Mayor*	Susan Brown
Riaz Rafique, *Labour councillor*	Paul Bhattacharjee
Joan Cummings, *Liberal Democrat Leader*	Kate Best
Roger Priestman, *Conservative Leader*	Tony Turner
Derek Morley, *Labour councillor*	Jonathan McGuinness
Barry Ings, *the Chief Executive*	Geoffrey Beevers

THE TOWN

Superintendent Bernard Ricks, *county constabulary*	Tony Turner
Yusuf Iqbal, *community leader*	Bhasker Patel
Michele Purdy, *a manicurist*	Caroline Strong
'Paula', *a manicurist*	Rebekah Staton
'Chloë', *a manicuree*	Helen Rutter
Reverend Tim Laundimer	Tony Turner
Michael Farrell, *a waiter*	Nick Fletcher
Sergeant Donald Baxter, *a community policeman*	Deka Walmsley
Mrs Chowdury, *a dignitary*	Sameena Zehra
'Bronwen', *a teenage prostitute*	Helen Rutter
Kurshid Hafiz, *Anwar's nephew*	Ranjit Krishnamma

Characters

Les Slater, *35, Britannia*
Shirley Honeywell, *30s, Britannia*
The Bishop
A White Schoolgirl
An Asian Schoolboy
An Asian Woman in a wheelchair
Britannia Supporter
Fazal Mansoor, *23*
Mrs Hatchard, *40s, hotel manageress*
Policeman
Policewoman
Shaz, *20s, reporter*
Sue Braithwaite, *20s, celebrity*
Asian Rioter
'Brad', *late 20s, country-and-western band*

THE INQUIRY

Usher
Lord Stanley, *50s, chair*
Jill Watts, *40s, barrister*
Ranjit Singh Khera, *33, barrister*
Transcribers

Citizens, Dignitaries, Members of the Public at the Inquiry, etc.

Doubling

Michele Purdy/Mrs Hatchard
Paula/Shirley Honeywell/Sue Braithwaite
Chloë/Bronwen/Schoolgirl/Transcriber/Shaz
Michael/Postman/Britannia Supporter
Mrs Chowdury/Leena Harvey Wells/Asian Woman
Fazal Mansoor/Chauffeur/Asian boy/Rioter
Superintendant Ricks/Tim Laundimer/Roger Priestman
Bob Stanley/Barry Ings/The Bishop
Waitress/Joan Cummings/Marjory/Policewoman
Usher/Joe McIntyre/Liberal Democrat/Policeman
Kurshid Hafiz/Ranjit Khera
Les Slater/Donald Baxter/Brad
The Mayor/Jill Watts

Setting

Apart from one scene in London, the play is set in and around a town in West Yorkshire, during an early term of a current Labour Government.

Notation

A dash (–) indicates that a character is interrupted.

A slash (/) indicates that the next character to speak starts speaking at that point (what follows the slash need not be completed, it is there to indicate the character's train of thought).

An ellipsis (. . .) indicates that a character has interrupted him or herself.

Acknowledgements

I am grateful to the many people who allowed me to interview them for *Playing with Fire*. I am particularly indebted to those whom I consulted several times, including Ted Cantle, Michael Frater, John Haward, Andrew Howell, Gwenda Hughes, Patricia Hughes, Sir Michael Lyons, Sue Moffat, Lisa O'Neill, Geoffrey Robertson QC, Kevin Shaw, John Stewart, and, as ever, the staff of the Institute of Race Relations.

D.E.

This text went to press before the end of rehearsals so may differ slightly from the play as performed.

'I want the message to local government to be loud and clear.

A changing role is part of your heritage. The people's needs require you to change again so that you can play your part in helping to modernise Britain and, in partnership with others, deliver the policies on which this Governme nt was elected.

If you accept this challenge, you will not find us wanting. You can look forward to an enhanced role and new powers. Your contribution will be recognised. Your status enhanced.

If you are unwilling or unable to work to the modern agenda then the Government will have to look to other partners to take on your role.'

Tony Blair, *Leading the Way:*
A New Vision for Local Government, 1998

'In relation to Poorly Performing Councils, the Government wishes Councils to achieve recovery by a process of voluntary cooperation that emphasises action by the Council, not the Government ... The principal role of the Lead Official is to advise Ministers on whether the Council has the will and the wherewithal to achieve recovery within an acceptable timeframe under its own steam, or whether Ministers should consider using statutory powers of intervention. Having said that, Lead Officials are in a position, by virtue of their role and experience, to offer informal advice, to question/critique Council plans and to act as a critical friend.'

Government Engagement with Poorly Performing Councils,
Office of the Deputy Prime Minister, November 2003

ACT ONE

Scene One

Empty stage. Enter ALEX CLIFTON. *She is 38.*

ALEX. OK. We had this joke about our tactics with the Council. We said, we'd try the Polish Strategy and if that didn't work we'd have to go for the Czechoslovak Option even if that risked the Indochina Syndrome, if not worse. But of course in all those cases we were talking about them – the Council – as a plucky little country, standing up for what they saw as right against the threat of having what another country wanted dumped on them from a great height. So what did that make us?

ALEX *looks round to see* OTHERS *walking onto the stage. First, a town hall* USHER:

USHER. Ladies and gentlemen, could you please switch off all mobile phones. Or pagers, bleepers *and* all mobile phones.

YUSUF IQBAL *is in his 40s:*

YUSUF. I am Yusuf Iqbal. I am Chairman of the Pakistani Welfare Group and the Secretary of Wyverdale Islamic Relief.

SUPERINTENDANT RICKS *is in his 50s:*

RICKS. I am Superintendant Bernard Ricks.

YUSUF (*afterthought*). And founder member of Broughton Moor Neighbourhood Association.

RICKS. And I should say at the outset that I was instructed to give evidence to this Inquiry.

YUSUF (*another afterthought*). Oh, and Governor of Broughton Girls.

MICHELE PURDY, *a woman of 41:*

MICHELE. 'These are my words as a woman who has lost her son to violence. But they are also words from the people of this town.'

Slight pause.

I think I should say 'the majority of people of this town'.

COUNCILLOR JACK ROSS, *46, Scottish:*

JACK. My name is Jack Ross and I am temporarily the Acting Leader – well, I am the Acting Leader – of the Labour Group on Wyverdale District Council, and as such I feel the need to set the record straight. As it seems the Council has become the whipping boy in this Inquiry.

And LORD STANLEY – BOB *– who is in his 50s:*

STANLEY. Good morning. My name's Lord Stanley and I am a barrister.

Correction:

My name's Bob Stanley and I am a barrister and member of the House of Lords. And I've been invited to inquire into and then report on the course and causes of the events of last April here in Wyverdale.

Enter GEORGE ALDRED, *51, Leader of Wyverdale Metropolitan Council. As he strides to the front of the stage, the* OTHERS *leave. It is quickly clear that* GEORGE *too is rehearsing:*

GEORGE. See, you know your trouble, Minister? It's the driving. I mean, you drive north, it's all rolling meadowland and the glories of the English countryside. While you take the train, you see things from t'other way about. Car parks, car graveyards, gardens, ginnels and what's dumped in 'em. Cool Britannia's Back Side.

The 'ping pong' that precedes a train announcement. This reminds him where he is, which is a train lavatory. He checks his fly, straightens his tie and has another go:

See, you know what, Minister? If I was you, I'd leave the car and take the train.

TRAIN MANAGER (*loudspeaker*). Ladies and gentlemen, I regret to announce that this train will arrive at King's Cross approximately 37 minutes late . . .

GEORGE *looks at his watch and shrugs.*

GEORGE. See, you know what, 'Stephen'?

Slight pause.

'Steve'?

Scene Two

A ministry building in London. STEPHEN CROFT *is 45, though with a boyish appearance. He is a junior minister in the Office of the Deputy Prime Minister.*

STEPHEN. Ah. Leader.

GEORGE *turns to see* STEPHEN.

GEORGE (*looking at his watch*). Minister, beg pardon . . .

STEPHEN *leading* GEORGE *into his office.*

STEPHEN. Don't worry. Frankly, that's the reason why I always take the car.

Now in his office, STEPHEN *goes to his desk and dials a number.*

GEORGE. But, see, you know what . . .

STEPHEN (*phone*). Yes, he's here. Can you find Alex, and then get us all some drinks?

He puts the phone down.

Forgive me, you were saying?

GEORGE *decides not to pursue this.*

GEORGE (*gesturing round*). Well. The Office of the Deputy Prime Minister.

STEPHEN. Well, not the, actual . . .

GEORGE. So who'd have thought it, eh?

STEPHEN. We thought it, George. But the real trick is thinking of it twice.

GEORGE. We was trying to work out, whether being summoned meant good tidings or bad tidings. For the citizens of Wyverdale.

STEPHEN. Well, that does beg the question, doesn't it?

STEPHEN doesn't look at GEORGE, but opens a report on his desk, and sits, gesturing to GEORGE to do the same.

GEORGE. Aha. So, what . . .

STEPHEN leafing through the document as he questions GEORGE.

STEPHEN. Now you got re-elected back in May?

GEORGE. Oh, ay.

STEPHEN. With a reduced majority.

GEORGE. A couple of Lib Dems.

STEPHEN. The far right did quite well in . . . Fenleydale and Thawston.

GEORGE. Didn't win owt.

STEPHEN. So you don't see Britannia as a problem.

GEORGE. No, we sees 'em as a joke.

STEPHEN. Well, let's hope you're right. And, structurally, you have a leader – that's you – and a cabinet?

GEORGE. That's right.

STEPHEN. You didn't hold a referendum on a mayor?

GEORGE. We've already got a mayor.

STEPHEN. Well, obviously I don't mean someone in a lacy ruff wearing chains and opening supermarkets. I mean an elected mayor with executive authority. As provided for by the Local Government / Act 2000.

GEORGE. We felt the citizens of Wyverdale didn't want the system / changing.

STEPHEN. Because we feel that robust, accountable and performance-driven governance is vital for the delivery of the modernisation agenda.

GEORGE. Ay, well, we have some trouble with the modernisation agenda.

STEPHEN (*tapping the report*). So you do.

GEORGE. And that'll be them nice young lads and lasses camped out in my office.

STEPHEN. The Audit Commission, yes.

GEORGE. Who as I understand it / are empowered . . .

STEPHEN. Who are required to rank a council's overall performance in one of five bands: excellent, good, fair, weak and poor.

GEORGE. And here's me thinking as we'd get a silver star.

STEPHEN. No, George, you don't get a silver star.

Enter ALEX CLIFTON *with* JOE McINTYRE, *30, who carries* ALEX's *coat. Seeing them enter,* STEPHEN *stands.* ALEX *puts down her briefcase.* GEORGE *looks round.*

Which is why we summoned you.

GEORGE (*looking back to* STEPHEN). This'll be Alex.

STEPHEN. It is. Joe, can you get us all a cup of tea.

GEORGE *gets up.*

GEORGE (*to* ALEX). Two sugars, love.

He puts his hand out to JOE:

George Aldred.

JOE. Joe.

Slight pause.

That's, with an 'e'.

GEORGE. Ah. Right.

ALEX. I'm Alex Clifton.

GEORGE. How d'you do.

Slight pause. STEPHEN *nods to* JOE, *who puts down* ALEX's *coat, and goes.*

ALEX. It's actually . . . quite an easy, um, mistake . . .

STEPHEN. I've given George the headline.

ALEX *picks up her case and goes to sit.*

ALEX. Of course the overall rating does tend to mask the good things.

STEPHEN. Of which there are some, obviously.

GEORGE. Look, has everybody read this bloody thing but me?

STEPHEN *hands over a copy, and sits.* ALEX *sits, opens her briefcase and takes out her copy.* GEORGE *sits too.*

I may need a couple more.

ALEX. It'll be on our website.

GEORGE. Well, that'll go down favourite on the Morrison estate.

STEPHEN. And we'd expect you to put it up on yours.

GEORGE. We're having problems with our website.

ALEX. Quite.

GEORGE. Maybe we were spending too much time putting central heating into all our housing. Or maybe your people didn't notice that.

STEPHEN. Yes, they did. But they also noticed that you didn't do a risk assessment, which is why you lost three contractors without compensation, and you didn't do a stock survey, so you were spending millions on heating houses that you'll have to knock down in three years. And of course it wasn't helped by your deplorable council-tax-collection rate.

GEORGE. Which weren't helped by you / capping us.

STEPHEN. But actually, George, your real housing problem's with the run-down private stock in the Asian area. That's, Broughton Park?

GEORGE. Broughton Moor. The Park's the football ground.

STEPHEN. Doing well, I hear.

GEORGE. But you know, we do tend to give priority / to our own stock –

ALEX. But you wouldn't have to pay for it. Broughton Moor is the 37th poorest ward in Britain. You could have bid for an S.R.B. for fabric, domestic improvement, landscaping, traffic calming *and* economic development and still had change.

GEORGE. Remind me, SRB is what? Sod All for Rotten Boroughs?

STEPHEN. Single Regeneration Budgets. It's a bit alarming that you don't know that.

GEORGE. I know what an SRB is.

STEPHEN. So why didn't you apply?

GEORGE. Like, we're not right keen on its competitive approach.

STEPHEN. So your bottom line is that the largely Asian citizens of Broughton Moor are denied new bathrooms and new roofs because you don't approve of getting out and batting for their interests. And our bottom line is that the overall performance of the Metropolitan District of Wyverdale is 'poor'.

GEORGE. So, what? You want my resignation?

STEPHEN. Absolutely not. And that's the first bit of good news.

GEORGE. Oh, what's the second?

STEPHEN. We've asked Alex to be the lead official in this case.

GEORGE. And . . . what, exactly . . . ?

STEPHEN. Officially, her function is to advise me if you have the will and wherewithal to achieve recovery. Or if we need to take you over.

GEORGE. And unofficially?

STEPHEN. To challenge, question and critique the drawing-up and implementation of a recovery plan sufficiently robust to obviate the necessity of that happening.

GEORGE. So it's kind of, Czechoslovakia and the Russians? You're not really invading us, we 'invite you in'?

STEPHEN. But we'd like to feel that as our representative she'd be treated with the openness and hospitality for which Wyverdale is famed.

GEORGE. So may I ask, with all due respect, if there is any evidence that Ms Clifton has the will and wherewithal to run a whelkstall?

GEORGE *looks at* ALEX, *who hands him a piece of paper.*
He reads it.

Women's Resources. Women's Support Unit. Press Officer,
SWAR. Oh, Stepney Women Against Racism. Institute for
Public Policy. Assistant, Deputy, oh, Head of Leisure
Services. Oh, that's somewhere else. Well, you folks move
about.

ALEX. There's a lot of London.

GEORGE. And Leisure would be what? 'The arts'?

ALEX. My background is in sport.

GEORGE. The martial arts, then.

ALEX. George, I started out in London local government in
the '80s. I did enough women's self-defence to last a
lifetime.

STEPHEN. Alex came 93rd in the 1987 London Marathon.

ALEX. And 47th in the Great North Run.

STEPHEN. So she knows her mushy peas . . .

GEORGE. From her guacamole.

STEPHEN. That's when she wasn't serving as Interim Chief
Executive of another – challenging authority.

GEORGE. Which she sorts.

STEPHEN. Triumphantly.

GEORGE. Well, champion.

STEPHEN. Proving her capacity to transform the most
demanding whelkstall.

GEORGE. So why din't she get the real job?

Gesturing at the paper:

Rather than leaving after six months as an interim and
joining something called 'Civitatis'. Which I take to be
some class of think-tank?

STEPHEN. From which we poached her to sort you.

Pause. GEORGE *decides not to press it.*

GEORGE. And she does her lead officialling on site?

ALEX. Not entirely, but I'd like to know a good hotel.

GEORGE. One of the audit people wanted somewhere with a sauna.

ALEX. I work up my own sweat.

GEORGE. The George it is.

STEPHEN. Uh, did they actually name a hotel after . . . ?

GEORGE. Royal Visit, 1922.

He stands.

Well, to the mercies of an outsourced railway.

ALEX. Look – George. I understand what it must be like. I've read the report. There's great stuff. Preschool. Disabilities. Actually, sport.

GEORGE. Well, thanks a bunch.

ALEX. But all that good is threatened by things that aren't so great. No senior-management appraisal or member training. No neighbourhood partnerships to combat antisocial public-space behaviours. No diversity criteria in place. Building projects set up without proper risk assessment and abandoned. Apparently, you don't know how many kids you've got in care. I mean, it really isn't arty-farty southern sushi-eating Shiraz-swilling poncy self-abuse to say that a conurbation of a quarter of a million deserves a council which can run a website.

GEORGE. Ay well. No doubt you'll put us right.

ALEX. But it isn't actually my job to / put you right –

GEORGE. Next to the Cabinet, I tell you, I'm a pussycat.

GEORGE *goes out, nearly bumping into the entering* JOE, *with a tray of teas.*

S'all right, I'm not stopping.

GEORGE *goes out.*

ALEX. Of course it isn't really Czechoslovakia. It's more like Poland. Do the job yourself or we take you over.

JOE (*to* STEPHEN). You've got Leena Harvey Wells from Habitus.

STEPHEN. I'll be a minute.

JOE *puts down the tea and goes.*

So you're sure you're up for heading north?

ALEX. My mum will be delighted. She can apply her principles of parenting at last.

STEPHEN. Because there's obviously a risk in sending you.

Slight pause.

ALEX. I'm sure that you've assessed it.

STEPHEN. The identikit lead official is a former Chief Exec possessed of wisdom, tact, and gravitas in the autumn of his days.

ALEX. At least it's time to change the pronoun.

STEPHEN. Immune to barracking from hostile terraces . . .

ALEX. Hey, bring it on.

STEPHEN. Tough on Wyverdale,

ALEX. tough on the causes of . . .

STEPHEN. But ever mindful that the cause that really matters is . . .

ALEX. . . . the cause you can address.

STEPHEN. And able therefore to locate and nurture and sustain those allies who will enable you to transform Wyverdale from poor to weak to fair to good. Or rather, to persuade it so to transform itself.

ALEX. Are you suggesting I can't make alliances?

STEPHEN. Alex, you should be Chief Executive of a major London borough.

ALEX. Yes?

STEPHEN. You should remember why you're not.

Pause.

ALEX. Well, so should you.

Slight pause.

STEPHEN. Which is why your getting this one right matters so much to us both.

JOE *has re-entered.*

JOE. Ms Harvey Wells has a four o'clock which she can't miss.

STEPHEN *looks at his watch.* JOE *tidies up the tea.*

In Waltham Forest.

STEPHEN. In fact, if you need a hard cop, Leena Harvey Wells might not be a bad idea.

ALEX. Well, quite.

STEPHEN. You realise, the problem with your arty farty speech.

ALEX. No, what?

STEPHEN. You told him what you wanted them to do.

ALEX. What's wrong with that?

STEPHEN. Because, by the time you've got there, they'll have done it.

He goes out.

ALEX. Fuck. Round One.

JOE. Round one to who?

ALEX. To Wyverdale.

JOE *goes out,* ALEX *turns out front, and the Ministry disappears.*

Scene Three

Downtown Wyverdale, late afternoon. The good CITIZENS *of Wyverdale swirl across the stage. A passing* CITIZEN – *who we'll later meet as the 59-year-old Labour councillor* FRANK WILKINS – *gives a helpful piece of information:*

FRANK. Comprising as it does the once proud independent boroughs of Broughton, Casterdyke and Fenleydale.

ALEX. Now with its pound shops, budget shops and charity pound budget shops and bargain booze and budget booze and Cash Cow used electrical.

Two manicurists – MICHELE PURDY *and the 27-year-old*
PAULA *– emerge from the swirl, with their client* CHLOË,
25.

CHLOË. And T.Rexstacy and Fabbarama at the Oddfellows.

MICHELE. And Bernard Manning at the Firth of Forth on
Friday –

PAULA. '*Not* for the politically correct . . . '

ALEX. And that's not to mention:

PAULA. Tanning, tanning, nails, tattoo . . .

MICHELE. And tanning.

CHLOË. Phone shop.

ALEX. Nail shop, hair stylist . . .

MICHELE. Tanning.

CHLOË. Beauty.

ALEX. Nails.

PAULA. See for us it's normal, only folk from down south
think it's queer.

ALEX. And having made my calls I find I have an hour to
kill . . .

MICHELE. And wanting summat doing with them hands like
urgently –

ALEX. I make my first mistake.

ALEX *is now in a nail shop, being manicured by* MICHELE
as PAULA *manicures* CHLOË.

MICHELE. We're doing a fiver off the French.

ALEX. I think, just basic.

PAULA. We can do you basic and fibreglass extensions or we
can drill you for a jewelled feature twenty pound all in.

ALEX. But even so.

MICHELE. Now our October specials this October are matt
moonlight, autumn mist, warm cherry frost and russet
beauty.

ALEX *splays her hands.*

ALEX (*out front*). And the cherry frost it was.

MICHELE. No seriously apparently there's this baby born in the silence before Elton John does 'Candle in the Wind' and she like didn't cry while it were over.

ALEX (*out front*). And I'm committed.

PAULA. No this global warning 'parently t'int cars'n'that it's actually the nuclear tests like in Pakistan.

ALEX (*out front*). And from Pakistan of course it's but a step . . .

MICHELE. And apparently like in Koran adultery's OK with any lass you like 'cept if she's Muslim.

ALEX. Um . . .

CHLOË. That's crap that is.

PAULA. And they eat donkeys.

ALEX (*hoping her nails are dry*). Um, is this . . .

MICHELE. No, petal, that's the base coat.

CHLOË. That's so crap.

PAULA. See she's only saying that like 'cos of who she's courting . . .

CHLOË. Eff off.

PAULA *and* MICHELE *both mouth 'Paki'.*

ALEX (*out front*). And I'm trapped there waiting for my base to dry.

MICHELE. Say you're stopping at the George?

ALEX (*out front*). Not only stopping but, so I'm informed, meeting with George Aldred in the Howard Suite at six.

As they go, CHLOË, MICHELE *and* PAULA *recite a poem drummed into them at school:*

ALL THREE.
'In shadow yet of Moor and Mill,
Its crags and flagstones blackened still.'

They're gone, as ALEX *turns into the next scene:*

ALEX. And there we were.

Scene Four

The Howard Suite of the George Hotel. A finger buffet laid out on a table. Some chairs, but currently the welcoming party is standing: it includes COUNCILLORS GEORGE ALDRED, JACK ROSS, *and* ANWAR HAFIZ *(50), community representative* YUSUF IQBAL, *community policeman* SERGEANT DONALD BAXTER *(40s), and* MRS CHOWDURY, *the* REVEREND TIM LAUNDIMER *and two other* GUESTS. *Enough people are smoking – including* YUSUF IQBAL *on his pipe – to make it noticeable.* ALEX *is taken aback – this isn't what she expected.*

GEORGE. Ah, Alex. Welcome to . . .

ALEX. A smoke-filled room.

Some people laugh. ANWAR HAFIZ's *mobile phone goes. He answers it, as a* WAITER *enters with a tray of drinks, beer, wine, juice and water. Later, we will learn he is* MICHAEL FARRELL.

GEORGE. Good journey?

ALEX. Well, I took the train.

Laughter.

GEORGE. Now, this is Jack Ross, Chair – I beg his pardon, Cabinet Member for Social Services.

ALEX. Ah, I'm pleased to meet you.

JACK (*food*). Bit of everything?

ALEX *gestures assent.*

GEORGE. And this is, Reverend, Tim . . .

TIM. Tim Laundimer. The Bishop couldn't make it, I'm afraid.

ALEX. Oh, dear.

GEORGE. Tim's parish includes Thawston.

ALEX. Oh, is that right?

TIM. Where the neighbourhood patrols are just beginning to make a real impact.

Nodding to BAXTER.

As Sergeant Baxter will confirm.

BAXTER. Oh, ay.

ALEX. I see.

Enter COUNCILLOR ARTHUR BARRACLOUGH, *in his late 60s, a substantial figure in all senses.*

ARTHUR. Ay up.

GEORGE. Ay up, Arthur, this is Alex Clifton.

ALEX. Well, hallo.

ARTHUR. Barraclough. I'm Housing. How do.

GEORGE. Who we named the new south stand at Broughton Park for.

ALEX. Oh, yes?

BAXTER*'s phone goes.*

BAXTER (*phone*). Donald Baxter.

ARTHUR. That's the football ground.

ALEX. Doing well, I hear.

ARTHUR. Last Saturday, we were lucky to get nil.

MICHAEL (*offering*). Uh, drink?

ALEX. Uh, is this dry?

MICHAEL. Dunno.

GEORGE *nods to* MICHAEL *to go.*

I'll check.

ALEX (*thinking she shouldn't drink*). In fact . . .

Rather quickly, MICHAEL *turns and heads out.* ARTHUR *takes a glass of beer as he passes. Enter* COUNCILLOR FRANK WILKINS, *who rather elegantly scoops up a glass of red wine from the exiting* MICHAEL.

FRANK. Good evening.

ARTHUR (*heading for the food*). Hallo, Frank.

Seeing JACK *moving in on* ALEX, GEORGE *goes to* ANWAR HAFIZ. JACK *brings* ALEX *her food.*

JACK. Presumably you read our end-of-term report?

ALEX. The assessment, yes.

FRANK WILKINS *looks on, a quizzical smile on his face.*

JACK. We don't agree with the idea we've got too many kids in care.

ALEX. But according to / the CPA –

JACK. Seeing how, as a proportion of the population, the three hundred and sixty-seven children and young people we were looking after as of lunchtime yesterday is less than many comparable authorities.

ALEX. I – right.

JACK'*s phone goes – his ringtone is* Mission Impossible, *but it's covered by* GEORGE *sweeping* ANWAR HAFIZ *to* ALEX.

GEORGE. And this is Councillor Hafiz.

JACK (*phone*). Jack Ross.

ALEX. How do you do?

GEORGE *spots the* MAYOR, COUNCILLOR MAUREEN TEALE, *entering with her* CHAUFFEUR.

ANWAR. I'm well. 'Stepney Women Against Racism'?

ALEX. Many years ago.

GEORGE. Ah, Madam Mayor.

ANWAR. And now you are sent to us by Mr Croft, MP for nearby Kirkle South.

ALEX. Well, if you like . . .

Acknowledging the MAYOR'*s apologetic shrug,* GEORGE *takes her arm to lead her over to* ALEX.

ANWAR. Where I believe the council-tax-collection rate is eight percentage points beneath our rate in Wyverdale.

ALEX (*turning to the approaching* GEORGE). OK. Look,
George . . .

GEORGE arrives with the MAYOR, *as* MICHAEL *re-
enters with his tray, on which is now an old-fashioned,
Babysham-style champagne glass.*

GEORGE. Now, Madam Mayor, I'd like you to meet Alex
Clifton.

MAYOR. I'm so sorry, I've been opening a Lidl up East
Thawston End.

ALEX. Just so.

MICHAEL. They don't have dry. But they do have fizzy.

ALEX. Actually, I don't think . . .

But the MAYOR *has taken* ALEX's *glass. She takes
another – why not?*

Thanks.

MAYOR. Of course, it in't all retail outlets, obviously.

ALEX. Obviously.

MAYOR. For example, last month I were privileged to open
our spectacular new north stand at Broughton Park.

GEORGE. South stand.

ALEX. Yeah, sure. George, what is going on?

She has said this loudly enough for most people to hear.

ARTHUR. Ay up.

GEORGE. What do you mean?

Now everyone is listening. Enter COUNCILLOR RIAZ
RAFIQUE, *a 39-year-old solicitor.*

RIAZ. Beg pardon. I . . . ah. Oh.

ALEX. I mean, I get what's going *on*, the precision of the
childcare figures, the achievements of the neighbourhood
patrols in Thawston, the excellence of the new stand at
Broughton Park, the fact that you have managed to come up
with one authority whose council-tax-collection rates are
actually worse than yours . . . But I mean, what's going on
this evening? With these people here.

GEORGE. We hoped you'd see it as the kind of hearty welcome for which Wyverdale is famed.

ALEX. Of course.

To TIM LAUNDIMER *and* BAXTER:

And I'm very pleased to have met you, and . . .

She gestures at YUSUF IQBAL.

YUSUF. Yusuf Iqbal.

ARTHUR. Pakistani Welfare.

GEORGE. And Islamic Relief.

YUSUF. And school governor.

JACK brings MRS CHOWDURY *forward, her hand outstretched:*

JACK. And Mrs Chowdury, / senior registrar . . .

ALEX. But this is my first visit, and I had assumed I would be meeting with the Chief Executive, senior officials, the Cabinet, and – I had hoped – representatives of the other parties, with all of whom I have urgent business to conduct.

An askance look about the opposition. ALEX, *shaking* MRS CHOWDURY*'s hand, speaking to the* NON-COUNCILLORS.

I look forward to another meeting soon.

TIM. Pleased to meet you.

He goes out. YUSUF IQBAL *has a brief word with* RIAZ *on his way out.*

MAYOR (*to* GEORGE). Uh, did I do that right?

GEORGE. Yes, Maureen.

The MAYOR *goes out with her* CHAUFFEUR. GEORGE *gestures to the somewhat bemused* MICHAEL *to follow her.*

Ta very much.

JACK takes the MICHAEL*'s tray before he goes, and puts it on the table.*

RIAZ. Now, if it's just the Cabinet . . .

GEORGE (*to* RIAZ *and* ANWAR). No, you're party, you stay. You too, and all.

ARTHUR BARRACLOUGH takes a chair and sits.

ARTHUR. Well, if we're meeting . . .

ALEX. Is there not . . . a proper meeting room in the Council offices?

The COUNCILLORS *look at each other.*

JACK. I'll go and try and sort one out.

ALEX. And the Chief Executive?

ANWAR. Mr Ings is currently on leave.

ALEX. So hasn't he been told to come back?

GEORGE. What, off his holidays?

ALEX. Because I think it's vital we identify the resources that you'll need to have in place to formulate the plan for your recovery.

JACK. I'll go and find a room.

JACK going out.

GEORGE. When you say 'resources'?

ALEX. Well, for example, for the recovery process, you'd need to assess if you had the optimum support capacities in-house.

ARTHUR. Oh, would we now?

Having stopped to listen, JACK *goes out, a private little smile on his face.*

ALEX. And in view of the current funding rounds and in the absence of your current Chief Executive, it would be prudent to get any application you might wish to submit formulated now.

ARTHUR. What's that in old money?

GEORGE. Regeneration aid for Broughton Moor.

ARTHUR. Oh, ay?

ANWAR. A fine idea.

ARTHUR. Now, I wonder, how you see the basic trouble there.

RIAZ. Well, of course the most . . .

ARTHUR *gestures* RIAZ *to be silent.* ALEX *realises she's being tested.*

ALEX. Well, on every indicator, it ranks among the poorest ten per cent of wards.

ARTHUR. And that'd be in, what, health and education . . . ?

ALEX. Well, from memory, the boys' school has the lowest GCSE pass rates in the county.

ARTHUR. But you don't think real trouble's with the girls.

RIAZ. You see, the / issue is –

ALEX. There's nothing wrong with Broughton Girls. In fact / it's pretty good –

ARTHUR. No, love, not that kind of girl.

Pause.

ALEX. So, what?

RIAZ. He means the prostitutes.

ALEX. The prostitutes?

ARTHUR. And kerb-crawlers and pimps and pushers. And the needles and the condoms in the street.

GEORGE. Or as the audit people put it, 'Antisocial public-space behaviours'.

ALEX *recognises the quote from the report.*

ARTHUR. What, you didn't know?

ALEX. No, I'm afraid I / didn't –

ARTHUR. Well.

ARTHUR *mimes shooting himself in the foot. Some of the* OTHERS *laugh.* ALEX *decides she has to fight back at once.*

ALEX. So do you have a strategy?

GEORGE. Do *we* have a strategy?

ALEX. Who else?

ANWAR. Well, the people who have the power to stop it.

ALEX. And that's . . . ?

FRANK. The police inform us that you'll never stamp it out.

ALEX. But surely . . .

Enter JACK.

Right.

JACK. Rod's on his way. He'll open up the parlour. It'll be ten minutes.

ARTHUR. 'Right.'

ARTHUR *stands, goes to the sandwiches and puts a pile on a serviette.*

We've had all this before. They come up here, tell us what wants doing, and bugger off back to London, leaving us to clear up muck they've left behind. Be the same with this one, shouldn't wonder.

He pockets the pile.

Ten minutes.

He goes out.

ALEX. Um, does everyone have copies of / the Corporate Performance Assessment?

GEORGE. I'll get them done and all.

GEORGE *goes out, followed by* ANWAR, RIAZ *and* JACK.

FRANK. Well, is one not reminded of the 15th verse of the 11th chapter of the Gospel according to St Mark.

ALEX. I beg your pardon?

FRANK. The expulsion of the money-changers from the temple. Or, in this case, the wheeler-dealers from the Howard Suite.

ALEX. Well, if you like.

FRANK. Of course, you didn't shoot yourself in the foot.

ALEX. Well, thanks.

FRANK. Which means, you do yourself a minor injury in order to avoid a major one.

ALEX. Well, quite.

FRANK. He meant, you scored an own goal.

ALEX *looks at* FRANK, *who smiles, puts out his hand.*

Frank Wilkins.

ALEX (*shakes*). Cabinet Member for Education.

FRANK *gets a glass of red wine and offers it to* ALEX.

FRANK. The red is reasonably palatable.

ALEX *shakes her head.*

So, did we measure up to expectations?

ALEX. What do you mean?

FRANK. North of England local government. Here be dinosaurs.

ALEX. Well, I thought I'd get the party line.

FRANK. Just not . . .

ALEX (*the buffet*). . . . this sort of party.

FRANK. And of course you're right. It's pretty hard to find a council-tax-collection rate that's worse than ours. You should try getting housing benefit.

Slight pause.

Another thing you should probably consider is demonstrating you can actually do something.

ALEX *thinks* FRANK *is offering an alliance. She decides to test this out.*

ALEX. Good tip. So, what's the problem?

FRANK. Isn't that what you're supposed . . .

ALEX. Well, if it's governance, what's wrong with an elected mayor with executive authority?

FRANK. The fear is, you'd end up giving the same people greater clout.

ALEX. What's wrong with that?

FRANK. Well, you couldn't find a nicer sort than George.

ALEX. But?

FRANK. One can't expect all three R's. But – as our Great Helmsman – it would help if he had one.

ALEX *looks askance.*

I betray my calling. I was a head teacher for ten years.

ALEX. You 'were'?

FRANK. I decided I'd be happier handing down directives than receiving them.

ALEX. And if George stood as mayor, he'd be elected?

FRANK. Wyverdale? A monkey in a red rosette.

ALEX. And do you see yourself as – helmsman?

FRANK. Oh, come come.

ALEX. Well, you raised the point. Who else?

FRANK. Come come again.

ALEX. Jack Ross?

FRANK. Now I wonder, should I tell you this?

ALEX. Why not?

FRANK. There is a skeleton in Jack Ross's closet.

ALEX. Is there?

FRANK. Ask yourself, why a firebrand Scottish socialist would exchange Strathclyde for Wyverdale.

ALEX. And what's the answer?

FRANK. Do you know, that in our last fourteen exchanges, every sentence that you've uttered's ended with a question mark.

ALEX. Oh, really?

They both smile.

FRANK. Let's say, Jack Ross is a conviction politician. It's just, his previous convictions are of a rather different character.

ALEX. When you say previous . . . ?

FRANK. Well, shall we say, antisocial public-space behaviours. And as you know, we have 'issues' with the nightlife in this town.

She sees JACK ROSS *entering, carrying a copy of the Audit Commission report, followed by* RIAZ.

Well, Jack.

JACK. They've got the parlour open. But the only photocopier we can get access to is in your office.

FRANK. Right.

JACK (*to* ALEX). Councillor Rafique will escort you to the venue.

ALEX. Thanks.

To FRANK:

And thanks.

FRANK. Of course, the other thing's reminding people that, however painful things may be, there's always a worse fate in store.

JACK *looks questioningly,* FRANK *smiles seraphically, and goes out.* JACK *looks to* ALEX.

ALEX. We were discussing commonly misused expressions.

JACK. Were you now.

JACK *goes out.* RIAZ, *with a gracious gesture:*

RIAZ. Please, this way.

ALEX. Well, charmed, I'm sure.

Picking up her briefcase, ALEX *has a thought.*

So what's your ward?

RIAZ. It's Broughton Moor. Why do you ask?

ALEX. I'm told that's all I do. What are you doing afterwards?

RIAZ. Uh – why?

ALEX. I'm told I need to check out the nightlife in this town.

Scene Five

Broughton Moor, late at night. ALEX *and* RIAZ.

RIAZ (*out front*). Which, after the meeting . . .

ALEX (*to* RIAZ). Well, I wouldn't describe it in all senses as what you'd actually call a *meeting*.

RIAZ (*out front*). . . . is what happened.

> *Enter* YUSUF IQBAL.

> (*To* ALEX.) This is Mr Iqbal. You met earlier.

ALEX. Pakistani Welfare.

YUSUF. Welcome here to Back Moor Lane.

ALEX. And this is the centre of . . .

YUSUF. 'The industry.'

ALEX. So where's the action?

> YUSUF *points.*

> It's a V-reg Honda Civic.

YUSUF. They are most often Ford Mondeos.

ALEX. Let's address 'The Council can't do anything.'

> *She looks towards the car.* YUSUF *and* RIAZ *have a quiet word as:*

> (*Out front.*) And I told them that I was about to effect entry to the vehicle by opening the driver's door and I guessed that a young lady in a state of relative undress would leave the Honda Civic at high speed and should be apprehended.

RIAZ (*out front*). Which is precisely what occurred.

> *A prostitute we'll call* BRONWEN *runs on, pulling her skirt up and her top down.*

BRONWEN (*seeing* RIAZ *and* YUSUF). Oh, shit.

> *She turns to go the other way, but is chased and grabbed by* RIAZ *and* YUSUF.

ALEX (*out front*). While I told the driver that his registration was V37 ROH and if he drove away that number would appear in the *Clarion* on Friday.

BRONWEN. What the frigging hell you doing?

ALEX (*out front*). And might I ask some questions while he dressed?

YUSUF. Now young lady please be still and calm please.

BRONWEN. This is bang fucking out of order, this.

ALEX (*out front*). Like, whether he had a normal circuit.

BRONWEN. Like are you fucking cops or what?

ALEX (*out front*). Whether he'd be put off by CCTV.

BRONWEN. 'Cos if you in't, I got some *serious* fucking issues / with the way you . . .

YUSUF. Don't be silly.

ALEX (*out front*). What he felt about the prospect of exposure, / and . . .

BRONWEN. I will have you fuckers *arsed*.

YUSUF. Now stay still please young lady.

ALEX (*out front*). And in general how he felt about sexually abusing someone clearly under half his age.

BRONWEN. *And* done for sexual assault and all.

ALEX (*out front*). And with that I sent him on his way.

She comes over to RIAZ, YUSUF *and* BRONWEN.

Good evening.

BRONWEN. So are *you* a fucking copper?

ALEX. No, I'm from the Office of the Deputy Prime Minister. So, did he pay you?

BRONWEN. No?

ALEX. Aha.

ALEX takes out her purse to find a banknote. BRONWEN *gets this and nods.* ALEX *gestures to the* MEN *to release her. They do.*

How old are you?

BRONWEN. Fuck off.

ALEX *putting the note away:*

Nineteen.

ALEX (*keeps holding the note*). Yeah, right. How much outstanding?

BRONWEN. A'n't been done.

ALEX. And substances?

BRONWEN. Don't do no substances.

ALEX. So what's wrong?

BRONWEN. Nowt's wrong.

ALEX. So what the fuck are you doing sucking strangers off in cars?

Enter KURSHID HAFIZ, 25.

(*Turning to the* OTHERS.) OK, let's take her in . . .

BRONWEN. OK, I got some issues with abuse.

ALEX. Smack?

BRONWEN *shrugs.*

KURSHID (*Punjabi*). Kee horiya? [What's going on?}

YUSUF (*Punjabi*). Ae kudi prostitute a. [This girl here is a prostitute.]

ALEX. How many cautions?

BRONWEN. Two.

KURSHID (*Punjabi*). Te dooji? [And the other one?]

YUSUF (*Punjabi*). Ae government aali a. [She's from the Government.] John Prescott.

ALEX. So if it meant not getting done next time, would you go to rehab?

BRONWEN. Not going to no hospital.

ALEX. A drop-in centre.

BRONWEN. Uh?

ALEX. You know, somewhere you can drop in, have a chat, maybe a kip. Facilities.

KURSHID. What's going off here?

BRONWEN. Like what facilities?

ALEX. Smears. Free condoms. Benefit advice. And maybe, classes.

KURSHID. Classes?

ALEX. Literacy. IT skills.

BRONWEN. Fuck off.

ALEX. Or self-defence.

BRONWEN. What, like Bruce Lee?

KURSHID. Excuse me, what is the position here?

ALEX. Does that appeal? Do you think, with the rehab, maybe talking about benefits and debts, d'you think that that might help you off the game?

BRONWEN. Don't need no literary skills.

ALEX. So where d'you live?

BRONWEN. Why ask?

ALEX. Because Detective Constable Rafique either takes you there or to the station.

BRONWEN. It's Bellevue Crescent, Thawston.

ALEX. Number?

BRONWEN. Can't he just leave me at the corner?

ALEX. Yes.

RIAZ (*nodding to* KURSHID). In fact, my friend here has a taxi.

BRONWEN. Your *friend*?

ALEX *hands the banknote to* KURSHID HAFIZ.

ALEX. And when he gets you there, you get what's left.

BRONWEN *is about to make an issue of this but changes her mind.* RIAZ *makes the 'phone me' gesture to* KURSHID.

KURSHID. Free condoms. And you teach 'em martial arts and all.

He takes BRONWEN *out.*

ALEX. What does he mean?

YUSUF. He means, you offer them a prize.

ALEX. So do the girls use flats?

RIAZ. Sometimes. The Morrison estate.

ALEX. And that's white, right?

RIAZ nods.

So is anyone enforcing tenancy agreements there?

RIAZ doesn't know.

And there's demand. The guy was interesting. I think the real buzz is eyeing up the wares. I reckon, block the cruising circuit, make a few streets no-through-roads, you'd seriously reduce the hit. But obviously the thing he's really scared of is his registration number in the paper.

RIAZ. We've tried the *Clarion.*

ALEX. Does the Council have a newspaper?

RIAZ. Talked about it.

ALEX. Quite. And 'The Council can't do anything.'

Pause.

I'd say, you pull your fingers out, get a few blokes writing down car numbers, you could have this sorted out by easter.

RIAZ. And of course the Council could use ASBOs.

ALEX. I'm sorry, you mean . . .

YUSUF. Antisocial Behaviour / Orders.

ALEX. Yes, I know what ASBOs *are.*

YUSUF. Because, once they are handed down an ASBO, if they don't / desist . . .

ALEX. . . . . it's another way of putting girls in jail.

Clearly ALEX *doesn't favour that strategy.*

YUSUF. And what is wrong with that?

RIAZ's phone rings.

RIAZ (*phone*). Hi there.

> RIAZ *moves away, talking. Pause.*

ALEX (*looking at watch*). I'm sorry. Pretty late.

YUSUF. Oh, wait for chucking-out time.

ALEX (*nod to* RIAZ). I was thinking of his wife and family. Yours too, of course.

YUSUF. Oh, Mr Rafique has no wife.

ALEX. Oh?

YUSUF. He's a widower. With a small baby. Quite recent, and most tragic.

ALEX. Ah.

> RIAZ *returns, having finished his call.*

RIAZ. He saw her go in the house.

ALEX. Well, good.

RIAZ. Now we must get you back to your hotel.

ALEX (*pocket*). I've got the cab card somewhere.

YUSUF (*getting out his phone*). No, we get you one of ours.

RIAZ. Mr Iqbal owns the company.

YUSUF (*handing over card*). Ace Cabs. White drivers won't come here.

ALEX (*gesture to where the Honda was*). Demonstrably.

RIAZ. Though, of course, our cabs go into Thawston. And sometimes, they get out.

> YUSUF *moves away, making his call.*

ALEX. And Thawston is the Morrison estate?

RIAZ. Well, it includes the Morrison estate.

ALEX. Which is where they . . . ?

RIAZ. If they have a flat. Otherwise, it's in the car, or else East Thawston Mill.

ALEX. Which presumably . . .

RIAZ. Closed in 1980.

ALEX. But, before that . . .

RIAZ. Oh, time was, it employed two thousand people. Before some different people came here from the Punjab to do the night shift and 'take British jobs away'.

ALEX. And now?

RIAZ. A different kind of night shift.

ALEX. Quite.

RIAZ. In fact, the Morrison estate has a quite distinguished history.

ALEX. Oh, yes?

RIAZ. It was opened by the then Prime Minister on the 15th of June 1966.

ALEX. How on earth do you know that?

RIAZ. It's an auspicious date.

ALEX. What, is that the World Cup?

RIAZ. No, my birthday.

ALEX. So where were you . . . ?

RIAZ. Finchley.

Slight pause.

But only just. I was conceived in Balagonj, Sylhet.

ALEX. I was conceived in Berkeley, California.

Slight pause.

RIAZ. So we are both playing away.

ALEX. Look, Riaz, it would help / if you . . .

RIAZ. . . . if I reported what had happened here to my colleagues.

ALEX. Quite.

Slight pause.

Frank Wilkins thought I ought to demonstrate that I can actually do something.

RIAZ. Ah. And when he said you should remind us there is always a worse fate in store . . . ?

ALEX. He meant, ' . . . than me'.

She sees YUSUF *returning.*

YUSUF. So what do you talk about?

RIAZ. The Morrison estate.

YUSUF. One must have some sympathy. Particularly for those who bought their flats. We have condoms in the streets, they have needles in their stairways.

RIAZ. And Harold Wilson said it was the New Jerusalem.

YUSUF IQBAL *nods off towards the arriving cab.*

YUSUF. 'We' have arrived.

ALEX (*out front*). Which in a real sense was what had happened.

She turns to RIAZ, *whose brow is furrowed, affecting distracted thought.*

What's the matter?

RIAZ. I am trying to imagine.

ALEX. What?

RIAZ. A worse fate than you.

ALEX (*with a seraphic smile*). Oh, easy.

Scene Six

Three weeks later. A landing in the Council House. A line of chairs, at one end of which sits ROGER PRIESTMAN, *a man in his 60s. Nearly at the other end is a middle-aged woman,* JOAN CUMMINGS, *eating sandwiches from a plastic box.* JACK ROSS *enters, with* LEENA HARVEY WELLS, *an Asian woman in her early 40s.*

RIAZ (*out front*). As, after many meetings –

ALEX (*out front*). – over several visits –

ALEX *goes out.*

RIAZ (*out front*). – it turned out to be.

JACK. Ah. Joan.

JOAN (*mouth full*). Jack.

JACK. This is Leena.

RIAZ. Harvey Wells.

RIAZ goes out.

JOAN (*standing, still mouth full*). I'm sorry. Joan Cummings.

LEENA. How do you do. Please, don't get up.

JOAN's mobile goes off – the ringtone is 'Tomorrow' from Annie. *She juggles sandwiches and gets to her phone, shrugging apologetically.*

JOAN (*phone*). Hallo.

Enter ALEX and GEORGE.

ALEX. Leena, I'm sorry. We lost you.

GEORGE. Alex, this is Councillor Joan Cummings, Leader of the Liberal Democrats.

JOAN CUMMINGS waves, still on her call.

ALEX. Yes, we met at full council.

JACK. And Roger Priestman, Conservative.

JOAN CUMMINGS ends her call.

GEORGE. You want cross-party dialogue, you've got it.

JOAN's phone goes again.

JOAN (*phone*). Hallo?

Enter DEREK MORLEY, a Labour councillor in his early 30s.

DEREK. They're still at it.

ALEX. Still at what?

GEORGE (*to ALEX*). North Central Area Committee's overrunning in our room.

ALEX. Oh, really?

JACK's phone goes. The ring is still the theme from Mission Impossible. *He answers it.*

JACK (*phone*). Hi there, Jack Ross.

GEORGE (*to* ALEX). You've not met Councillor D. Morley.

DEREK. I been on me holidays.

ALEX. How do.

He shakes hands with ALEX.

LEENA. So there's a problem with the room?

ALEX. Welcome to Wyverdale. How's the hotel?

LEENA. It's fine.

GEORGE. So what about the parlour?

LEENA. Though if I have the need to come again . . .

JACK. Duke of Edinburgh Awards.

LEENA. . . . is there somewhere with a sauna?

Everyone hears this.

GEORGE (*gesturing to the chairs*). Well, seeing how much all of this is costing us . . .

LEENA. You mean . . . ?

ALEX. Well, if the alternative is a wasted evening . . .

JOAN. We could make a start.

LEENA. Uh, can we form a kind of semi-circle?

Looks to each other, but then PEOPLE *form the chairs into a kind of semi-circle. As they start, someone's phone goes, with the usual default tone.*

(*To* JOAN.) I'm sorry. October's always packed. I couldn't make it before now.

GEORGE. Don't fret. Ms Clifton's kept us at it.

GEORGE *realises it's his phone, and answers it.*

(*Phone.*) Later.

JACK. Went on a course once. Teamwork exercise. Room full of chairs, three groups, contradictory instructions. One was told to put them in a circle, another turn them upside down, the third, take 'em all next door. And the idea is to work out how the three groups might collaborate.

GEORGE (*phone*). I'll call you back.

JOAN. So did it work?

JACK. Well, it wasnae that great for the chairs.

DEREK. Or happen we'll have painting.

The semi-circle is more or less organised. DEREK's phone goes – his ringtone is 'The Red Flag'. He takes the call, moving away.

(*Phone.*) Wyverdale Infants?

ALEX. No, there won't be painting. Nor holding hands nor getting in touch with your inner child.

She waits for relief.

Now that we are broadly in agreement on the nature of the problems we face here in Wyverdale – I used the words 'broadly' and 'agreement' loosely – it's time to talk about the plan for your recovery. Particularly those elements on which – how can I put this? – full ownership has yet to be achieved. And who is Leena? Well, at present she's head honcho of a company called Habitus which provides advice and training and is indeed extortionately expensive, which is why we need to get full value from her time. And before that, she was Chief Executive of a Midlands District Council I won't name but where she gained her reputation for turning basket cases into showcases.

A ripple of disquiet, which ALEX has deliberately provoked. DEREK returns to the semi-circle.

But as Wyverdale is far from being anything remotely like a basket case, I'd imagine we'll be in the Fleece by nine.

LEENA. Thank you. Now, I'd normally do this with a PowerPoint, but . . .

ROGER. Welcome to Wyverdale.

LEENA. Now you're obviously disappointed with your grade. Who wouldn't be. But I always remind people of the Chinese proverb: 'Make the obstacle the path.'

Some disquiet.

And as we – well, you – prepare the plan that will bring about recovery, of course there will be bread-and-butter things like setting targets, getting that council-tax-collection rate up, getting those repair times down. And making sure that those performance indicators are really SMART.

She is hoping for a quiver of recognition. ALEX *prompts:*

ALEX. Specific, Measurable . . .

JOAN. Appropriate?

ROGER. Achievable.

LEENA. Well done. And 'R' is . . .

DEREK. Writ?

LEENA. Rit?

ALEX. Written.

LEENA. Um . . .

ALEX. Or, actually Relevant.

LEENA. And 'T' is . . .

JACK. Tiresome?

LEENA. Timed.

A couple of PEOPLE *snap their fingers, as if to say 'of course'.*

But however SMART, the crucial thing, in my experience, is making sure your corporate priorities deliver the three Es – that's Economy, Efficiency, Effectiveness . . .

Looks are exchanged.

. . . while remaining in alignment with your basic themes, your core vision and your strategic goals.

Pause.

DEREK. A question.

LEENA. Yes?

DEREK. Refuse collection.

LEENA. Yes?

DEREK. Is that a goal or a priority?

JOAN. Or indeed a theme.

LEENA. Well, obviously, service delivery would be among
your key priorities.

DEREK. 'Among.'

LEENA. And customer focus is demonstrably a theme.

*She's won a little ground but needs to look at her notes to
get herself back on track.*

But what I say to members is that the crucial driver of the
whole strategic plan is you. Which is why, as Alex says, it's
vital you have total buy-in from the start.

*Slight pause. ROGER PRIESTMAN's phone rings. It's
'Greensleeves'.*

ROGER (*phone*). Yes?

LEENA. Which brings us on to member training.

JACK. Uh . . .

ALEX (*out front*). At which point Leena Harvey Wells
informed the group that at Habitus they offer . . .

LEENA. . . . a series of developmental modules, called the
Modern Member programme.

JOAN. Which, covers what, exactly?

LEENA. Well, our foundation module embraces seven basic
member competencies. That's things like leafleting,
surgeries, community participation . . .

ROGER. You want to teach us how to conduct surgeries?

ALEX (*out front*). The Conservative inquired.

LEENA. And then there are competencies in scrutiny, best-
value obligations . . . Obviously in Wyverdale, diversity.
And sometimes we find members aren't aware of
appropriate relationships with officers.

ALEX. Often we find . . .

DEREK. Appropriate relationships?

*Enter the North Central Area Committee, including
FRANK, RIAZ, ANWAR, ARTHUR, a LIBERAL
DEMOCRAT and OBSERVERS from the general public,*

including LES SLATER, SHIRLEY HONEYWELL *and a* POSTMAN, *who is keen to lobby* JOAN CUMMINGS.

ALEX (*out front*). And then the North Central Area Committee entered, right on cue.

JACK. Appropriate in what respects?

LEENA (*seeing the* PEOPLE *coming in, with a look to* ALEX). Well, I . . .

ALEX *shrugs.*

ARTHUR. What's going off?

ALEX (*out front*). Including, as I didn't realise immediately, some members of the general public.

LES (*to* GEORGE). Evening, Councillor.

ANWAR HAFIZ*'s phone goes – his ringtone is 'I Will Survive'.*

ANWAR (*phone*). Hallo?

JACK (*to* LEENA). Go on.

ANWAR (*phone, Urdu*). Hanji. Assalam-o-alaikum. [Yes. May peace be with you.]

LEENA. Well, I think that sometimes councillors, for the best of reasons, tend to micro-manage.

DEREK. Oh?

ARTHUR. Ay up, George.

ARTHUR *gestures to* GEORGE, *who gets up, goes over and talks to him.* ROGER PRIESTMAN *switches on his phone and makes a call. This as:*

ANWAR (*Urdu, phone*). Nahi yaar Thursday nahi chalega. [No, I can't do Thursday.]

LEENA. You know, senior officers having hour-long meetings about library charges or hedge-trimming . . .

The LIBERAL DEMOCRAT *takes a chair, sits down behind* JOAN CUMMINGS *and talks to her. The* POSTMAN *joins in the conversation.*

JACK. Well, I'm sure we'd want to put a stop to *that*.

ALEX. Look, maybe we should . . .

DEREK. And the 'best-value obligation'?

LEENA. Well, it's the application of the four Cs.

ANWAR (*Urdu, phone*). Shukria ji. [Thanks.]

ARTHUR. The four whats?

DEREK. Please, do remind us.

ANWAR (*ending his call, Urdu*). Achchha. Khuda hafiz. [OK.
   May God be with you.]

   As ANWAR *ends his call, the* LIB DEM*'s phone rings,
   which he answers, standing.*

LEENA. Well, as you know . . .

LIB DEM (*phone*). Hey, Tom?

JOAN. If that's Tom Armitage, I want to speak to him.

LEENA. . . . it's Consult, Compare, Compete . . .

ALEX. And Challenge.

ARTHUR. And conspire, confuse . . .

DEREK. And what does the application of the four Cs tend to
   lead you to?

GEORGE. Well, maybe, now we've / got the room . . .

JACK. Apart, that is, from selling off our services to private
   companies.

LEENA. Well, no, I don't . . .

DEREK. Which I guess means, as we're not to badger busy
   officers . . .

JACK. . . . nor challenge our corporate priorities . . .

DEREK. . . . that the Modern Member's function is to turn up
   once a year, hand out the contracts . . .

JACK. . . . and then bugger off home.

   JOAN *takes the* LIB DEM*'s phone, to talk to Tom Armitage.*

ARTHUR. What are we discussing?

JACK. Member training.

ARTHUR. Ah.

ARTHUR's phone goes. His tone is 'The Ride of the Valkyries'. He answers it.

(*Phone.*) Barraclough.

JACK. In fact, in the spirit of open government, I'm sure we'd all love to know how a member-training session might actually work.

ALEX. For example, in diversity.

JOAN's phone goes. She answers it, so now she has two phones, one to either ear.

JOAN (*phone*). Hallo?

LEENA (*against her better judgement*). Well . . . to start with, I'd ask people to introduce themselves and say why they're there and what they hope to get out of the session.

LES *laughs.*

ARTHUR (*puts his hand over the phone*). Well, I'm A.R. Barraclough and I've been on the Wyverdale District Council and its predecessors for a quarter of a century and I'm here because three thousand seven hundred and fifteen people voted for me on the 5th of May.

(*Phone.*) Hallo, beg pardon.

ALEX. Yup. And the other thing she'd do to start with is to ask people to switch off their phones. Not as a courtesy to her, though it would be, but as a courtesy to your fellow councillors. And she might suggest things might go better if you didn't talk among yourselves.

By now JOAN has ended her calls.

SHIRLEY. Particularly in Urdu.

People turn to look at SHIRLEY.

ARTHUR (*phone*). Mo, I'll call you back.

He ends the call.

ALEX. Or displayed the slightest interest in improving the service you provide to those three thousand people who elected you.

To SHIRLEY:

I'm sorry, you were saying?

GEORGE. I should say, that this in't a councillor, / it's a member –

LES. And 'diversity' is racism awareness?

ALEX *gives an affirmative shrug as* GEORGE *tries to intervene:*

GEORGE. And in fact this is a private / meeting –

SHIRLEY. What, like, in a corridor?

LES. 'Cos I heard somewhere up the valley they had some coloured lady up from London saying as white people look more like monkeys than black people. That went down a treat.

Reaction.

Oh, beg pardon. I'm a general public. Silence at the back.

LEENA *gathers her papers and puts her coat on as she speaks.*

LEENA. Well, diversity includes racism awareness, obviously, but you'd want to look at other things. For example, in your case, the staggeringly low number of black and minority ethnic people in the Council workforce. And as language plays a part in that, I rang your Human Resources department – I think you call it 'Personnel' – and asked if there was anyone who spoke Punjabi. And they reacted as if I'd asked if they could put me through to the Planet Zog. But then, when I popped into Housing, it was made crystal clear to me by a very friendly woman that I would be much happier *not* living on the Morrison estate, which may of course be true. And wouldn't it be nice – I don't know, a Mandela Street? Or a grant to the Pakistani Welfare? Just something to acknowledge there's an ethnic population here at all?

Going out:

If you want to talk about recovery, I'll be . . . I'm not sure where.

GEORGE. The George.

UNIVERSITY OF WINCHESTER
LIBRARY

ALEX (*standing*). I'll take you over.

GEORGE. No, I'll take her. After all, she is our guest.

LEENA looks at GEORGE in surprise, but allows herself to be ushered out. A moment, then:

ARTHUR. Now, shoot me down in flames on this . . . but are we sure Wyverdale is ready for Ms . . .

DEREK. Harvey Wells.

JACK. Well, certainly, we made the path the obstacle.

To DEREK:

You coming, Comrade?

DEREK. Ay.

DEREK, ARTHUR and JACK go out, followed by the OTHERS, all of whom try to avoid eye contact with LES or SHIRLEY, who are left behind with ALEX, RIAZ and FRANK.

FRANK (*to ALEX*). Mission accomplished.

ALEX (*with a sideways glance at RIAZ, to stop him acknowledging he knows what's going on*). Quite.

RIAZ smiles, does the 'phone me' gesture to ALEX, and goes.

FRANK. Top marks.

He goes out, nodding briskly at LES and SHIRLEY. ALEX is following, to speak to RIAZ, when LES speaks.

LES. Good evening.

ALEX. Evening.

Slight pause.

So you're the general public?

LES. Sort of. And you're the white knight they've sent up to sort us out, like?

ALEX. Sort of.

SHIRLEY. Rather you than me.

ALEX. And when you say you're 'sort of' / general public . . .

LES (*hand out*). I'm Les Slater, last year's Council candidate for Thawston. Shirley Honeywell, ditto, Fenleydale.

ALEX (*as he puts her hand out to* LES). Oh, and what party?

ALEX *shakes* LES*'s hand just as* SHIRLEY*'s phone goes – her ringtone is 'There'll Always Be an England'.*

Ah.

SHIRLEY (*phone*). No, love, we're done.

End call.

LES. Britannia. Force of Darkness. Only two hundred short in Fenleydale and all.

SHIRLEY (*hand out to* ALEX). How do.

LES. See, she thinks we're skinheads with tattoos.

Enter GEORGE *as* ALEX *shakes* SHIRLEY*'s hand.*

GEORGE. Well, hallo, Mr Slater.

LES. Councillor. I think you owe me a letter about why you're banning English flags on council buildings.

GEORGE. 'll be in my in-tray. In the corner of the room.

LES (*to* ALEX). Red flag's all right, see. They used to call it the Socialist Republic.

SHIRLEY. Islamic Republic now, more like.

LES. You don't sort that, you've sorted nowt. Just so you know.

LES *and* SHIRLEY *go out.*

GEORGE. So you met the Munsters.

ALEX. Yes. A problem?

GEORGE. No, a joke. So what were that about?

ALEX. The Munsters?

GEORGE. No, the evening.

ALEX. I might ask the same of you.

GEORGE. I'd supposed it were some class of test.

ALEX. Well, if it was, you failed it.

GEORGE. So, what, you'll be sending in the tanks?

ALEX. You think we won't?

GEORGE. You think Stephen Croft wants to run Wyverdale?

ALEX. If necessary.

GEORGE. Unless we do what you want us to do.

ALEX. No, George. Not what 'we' want you to do.

GEORGE. Oh, for 'the people who elected us'.

ALEX. Of all classes, ethnic origins and genders.

GEORGE. Oh, what's that supposed to mean?

ALEX. Yesterday I visited the Broughton Neighbourhood Centre to tell them I'd been kerb-crawled by a Y-Reg Citroën Relay owned by 'ABC Locks, large enough to cope but small enough to care.' I think they sort of said that I should see it as a compliment.

GEORGE. Ay, well. We're on to that.

ALEX. You are?

GEORGE. Since your adventure down Back Moor Lane, Councillor Rafique has found a European fund for micro-something-ing areas of multiple etcetera. He reckons we could 'nest' an anti-prostitution package into that.

ALEX. Well, does he now?

GEORGE. The only problem being, as we'd have to match / that money with –

ALEX. So you've put in a bid?

GEORGE. Not really my job.

ALEX. So whose job is it?

GEORGE. Chief Executive.

ALEX. I thought that Mr Ings was on his holidays.

GEORGE. No, he's back.

ALEX. He's *back*? So why haven't we / been –

GEORGE. He's off sick.

ALEX. Sick?

Pause.

George. Statistically, you have the third worst rate of sickness leave in the north of England. Anecdotally, the state of the Council car park on Friday afternoons and Monday mornings might provide an explanation.

GEORGE. So you're suggesting / Barry Ings –

ALEX. Which is of course one reason why . . .

She stops herself.

GEORGE. Which is one reason what?

Pause.

Which is one reason you invited Leena Harvey Wells.

ALEX. I asked you to invite her because you obviously need somebody to help you draft the plan.

GEORGE. And that's the only reason?

ALEX. Is it beyond the bounds of possibility for Wyverdale to have a woman Chief Executive?

GEORGE *takes out his mobile phone.*

GEORGE. There in't a vacancy.

As GEORGE *dials.*

ALEX. So, what's this? We wax sentimental for a loyal if perennially absent public servant?

GEORGE. So what's wrong with / loyalty?

ALEX. George, please don't make a phone call.

GEORGE (*stops dialling*). Then you'll just have to believe me.

ALEX. About what?

GEORGE. About Barry Ings' arthroscopy. And its great success.

ALEX. I see.

GEORGE. In fact, he could be out in the morning.

ALEX. Good. But that doesn't mean that you don't have a problem.

GEORGE. No. But it shows there is a politics to this.

ALEX. I'm here to help with that.

GEORGE. Well, one way of helping would be chopping out the three Es and the four Cs and the seven basic competencies.

ALEX. Well, I hear you on the acronyms.

GEORGE. Also, if we're talking racial harmony in Wyverdale it would help if you stopped dispersing asylum-seekers here without telling us.

ALEX. I'm sorry?

GEORGE. 'Cos we say they can't be asylum 'cos we'd know. But then we're told Vic Square is chock-a-block with young lads with designer mobile phones and funny accents chatting up the lasses.

ALEX. George, what is a 'designer mobile / phone'?

GEORGE. And Frank Wilkins says his schools are stuffed with kids from Kurdistan and Africa who've been put in private housing here by Kent County Council. And while I'm all for providing a safe haven for those fleeing persecution, last weekend we had two hundred away-fans rampaging through the centre shouting 'If you want to kill a Paki, clap your hands', and if we want Britannia to *become* a problem that'll do just favourite. So, you know what? Happen not right now.

ALEX. I see your point. I'll do my best.

Pause.

But pretty soon I have to tell the minister you've got the will and wherewithal to run this – whelkstall. And currently I'm not convinced you have.

GEORGE. Tell me. Is there any one event – political event – that made Alexandra Clifton what she is?

Pause.

ALEX. You show me yours, I'll show you mine.

GEORGE. The 1974 coalminers' strike. Which brought in the three-day week and brought down the Heath Government. And we felt, could have brought about a revolution.

ALEX. But it didn't.

GEORGE. No. Yours?

ALEX. Live Aid. Because – in a way – it did.

GEORGE. Not 'SWAR'?

ALEX. Not 'SWAR'.

GEORGE. Didn't have you down as peace and love and rock and roll.

ALEX. Why not?

GEORGE. No, I had you down as someone who'd drag someone up from London, and then drop her in it, just to show us as there's summat worse than you.

Pause.

ALEX. So you think that's why / I brought . . .

GEORGE. And so does she.

Pause.

ALEX. So, then, do we have a deal?

GEORGE. A deal?

ALEX. A robust, coherent plan for Wyverdale's recovery. Replete with vision, goals and key priorities. In place by Bonfire Night.

She puts her hand out to GEORGE.

GEORGE. You know, I'll have to sell it to the Labour Group.

ALEX. Well, George, you're the politician.

They shake.

I ought to call her.

GEORGE. Ay. You ought.

She turns to go, then back:

ALEX. Oh, one more thing. Jack Ross.

GEORGE. On form tonight and no mistake.

ALEX. Well, quite. Does he have ambitions?

GEORGE. He's a Scottish member of the Labour Party.

ALEX. But of course, he couldn't do your job.

GEORGE. You might tell him that.

ALEX. Because he's got a criminal conviction.

GEORGE. Oh, ay?

ALEX. Ay. For something properly regarded as sexual abuse, in Glasgow.

GEORGE. So who d'you hear that from?

ALEX. I couldn't say.

GEORGE *gives an impatient shrug, turns to go.* ALEX, *in for a penny:*

But it struck me . . . one quite simple way of making Wyverdale's minority ethnic population visible . . . would be for your Cabinet to reflect it. Which would require the creation of a vacancy.

Slight pause.

GEORGE. Do you have anyone in mind?

ALEX (*obviously*). Jack Ross.

GEORGE. For the replacement.

ALEX. So how d'you think that Councillor Rafique found out about his European Fund?

GEORGE. He said he Googled it.

ALEX. Well, there's your answer.

Slight pause.

Unless you think that Wyverdale isn't ready for an Asian / Cabinet member –

GEORGE. Of course, it in't you wanting us to do what you want us to do.

ALEX. No, it isn't.

GEORGE. That'd be easy. You want summat different. You want us wanting it. You want us thinking as it's right.

ALEX. I do.

GEORGE. Like Councillor Rafique.

ALEX *says nothing.*

And if Leena Harvey Wells or Barry Ings or Jack needs dropping in it to achieve that, that's OK and all.

He goes out. RIAZ RAFIQUE *enters, and speaks out front.* ALEX *watches him a moment before she turns and goes. Although* RIAZ *doesn't use a phone, he's on one:*

RIAZ. Alex? It's Riaz. Well, I guess it would have to be the Silver Jubilee.

And I'm eleven, and my sister's five, and our shop's attacked by what my mother calls the bald boys from the NF or the BM or the something and we're sent upstairs to hide beneath our parents' bed for safety.

And the next day when the police are finished telling us it's only kids, we are visited by three members of the Anti-Fascist Anti-Racist this or that, and one is Asian Youth Whatever and the other two are women and the Workers' something else . . . And they say they'll stop outside the shop while we've got it boarded up and if we're attacked again, we've just to call them and they'll be straight round.

But most importantly, I'm underneath my father's bed, and I find his emergency store. Which is a battered suitcase, put there in case of civil uprising or industrial collapse or nuclear catastrophe. And in it there's Carr's Water Biscuits, Military Pickle, Marmite, Ovaltine, and Coleman's English Mustard in a tube.

Why do you ask?

Enter ALEX, *en route to the next scene:*

ALEX (*out front*). And shortly after Bonfire Night, a meeting was arranged in the Edward the Eighth room, aka Last-Chance Saloon. In the presence of the minister.

She joins the next scene.

Scene Seven

Three weeks later. The Council House: the Edward the Eighth Suite. A big table, currently with STEPHEN CROFT *sitting at it. As she joins him,* ALEX *switches off her phone. She puts it down on the table.* STEPHEN *looks at his watch.*

STEPHEN. What's the delay?

ALEX. Labour Group Meeting.

STEPHEN. Which is considering the plan due on November 5th.

ALEX. Which is considering the key goals and priorities of the plan which up until three weeks ago had no prospect of existing.

STEPHEN. Until you threatened them with Leena Harvey Wells.

ALEX. Well, quite.

STEPHEN. Plain sailing.

ALEX. Fingers crossed.

STEPHEN. No?

ALEX. Which is why you're here, to underline the fact that if they try and backtrack, then the tanks roll in three days.

STEPHEN. Well, surely, but . . .

Rather suddenly, enter GEORGE, FRANK, JACK, ANWAR, RIAZ, ARTHUR, DEREK, *with* MARJORY, *a secretary, and* BARRY INGS, *40s, the Chief Executive, currently on crutches. As everyone sits:*

Ah. Leader.

GEORGE. Minister. You'll not have met Barry Ings.

He gestures BARRY *to* STEPHEN.

ALEX. Chief Executive.

STEPHEN (*to* BARRY). No, indeed. I'm Stephen Croft.

With a little difficulty, BARRY *leans over to shake* STEPHEN's *hand:*

BARRY. Hallo.

GEORGE. Stephen, beg pardon. We were going through some matters with the group. Otherwise we'd have laid on summat more hospitable by way of welcome.

STEPHEN (*demurring*). I'm en route to my constituency.

JACK. Just dropping by to check we're eating up our greens.

GEORGE (*to* MARJORY). In fact, might there be tea?

STEPHEN. No, really it's . . .

GEORGE. I doubt you'll be the only taker.

MARJORY *goes out.*

ALEX. Minutes?

GEORGE. Jack'll do the honours while Marjory gets back.

ALEX. Good, but I meant the group.

GEORGE. Derek's laptop. Being printed as we speak.

This worries ALEX.

STEPHEN. Leader, as I see it, the purpose of this meeting . . .

ARTHUR. . . . is to call time. At Last-Chance Saloon.

STEPHEN. Well, yes . . .

GEORGE. Apologies for lateness. Group is always summat of a roughhouse. However, we're able to report that UNISON are willing to explore the implications of discussing multiskilling Housing department reception staff.

STEPHEN. Are 'willing to explore'?

GEORGE. Also, we raised member training, once again, which led to a certain amount of merry banter. some concerns from members who go back to Sexism Awareness classes, purging Noddy from the libraries and banning 'Baa Baa Black Sheep'.

ALEX. Well, I trust you reassured them.

JACK. Ay, on that score.

ALEX. And?

GEORGE. And – or but – the real questions were services, employment and the budget.

STEPHEN *looks quizzical.* ALEX, *concerned, rifling through her paperwork:*

ALEX. And you presented the 2nd of November / draft –

GEORGE. There was of course considerable sympathy for ensuring that our labour force is fully drawn from Wyverdale's diverse communities. But as was pointed out, we can't very well do that if we're – downsizing – our existing workforce simultaneously.

JACK. Or farming out our tax-collection service or our refuse or our parks to firms in Leeds or Manchester.

GEORGE. Well, ay.

Pause. STEPHEN *throws a glance at* ALEX.

ALEX. Um . . .

GEORGE. 'Cos as were pointed out, this in't Haringey or Tower Hamlets. This in't people working here for one week and someplace else as summat else the next and then it's off to Civitatis. Here, there's folk in ground maintenance and parks whose grandfathers worked for Council, back when it were Broughton, Fenleydale and Casterdyke. And, of course, since they shut the mills, we're by far the largest employer in the town.

STEPHEN *flashes another look at* ALEX.

So dragging in consultants on six hundred pound a day to send our loyal workforce off to sell Big Macs or sit in call centres or more likely end up doing nowt at all . . . in't an easy sell. But forgive me. I wax sentimental.

Slight pause.

So, in order to achieve a three-percentage-point / improvement in our council-tax-collection rate –

ALEX. No, I'm sorry, I can't deal with this.

She stands, packing her papers away.

You've had the best part of two months. During which advice has been consistently rejected. There have been constant prevarications and delays. After which, I am not having merry banter about banning Big Ears. I am not having Spanish practices in housing / maintained –

ARTHUR. 'Spanish / practices?'

GEORGE *gesture: 'Let her have her say.'*

ALEX. – maintained by unions who've taken five weeks to agree to *talk about* the fact that your customers can queue up to *three hours* to see someone who can deal with housing benefit but can't deal with rents. And while I'm just as moved as anybody else by . . .

Slight pause.

You know, it's not an *option*. You know, if you don't do something with your budget, Barry Ings will *have* to stop the Council changing lightbulbs or employing temporary staff or even burying the dead. And I'm not going to let that happen, George. So if there is not a cogent, robust and approved draft of a feasible Best Value Performance Plan to test, challenge and where necessary outsource your lamentable core services in place by 5.00pm on Friday, then under Section 15 of the Local Government Act 1999 I will impound your office and your car keys and I'll have you all sent home.

Pause. JACK *looks up from his minutes.*

JACK. Like, with a note?

A sudden clatter as MARJORY *enters with a rattling trolley of tea, crockery and biscuits.*

ARTHUR. Ah. Tea.

GEORGE. Thanks, Marjory.

STEPHEN *realises there's something wrong.*

STEPHEN. George, what was decided at the meeting?

GEORGE *stands, goes to the trolley, pours teas, and takes them round. As this happens,* MARJORY *sits and opens her notebook.*

GEORGE (*to* STEPHEN). Sorry, your rule. Give the bad news first.

Pouring tea:

And while it would be champion if someone . . . if there were a hint, that happen there might be a different . . . But, hey, there we are.

He takes a cup of tea to DEREK.

Derek. Members.

ALEX. What is this?

DEREK (*reads*). Following consultation with comparable authorities, we have 'engaged the services of a member-training and development provider'.

GEORGE. Arthur, Housing.

ARTHUR (*reads*). 'Acknowledging that our current policies and practices might unwittingly promote and/or perpetuate de facto residential segregation', we'll be changing the criteria 'to obviate that risk'. Whatever, 'obviate' might . . .

GEORGE *is continuing to serve tea.*

GEORGE. Frank, sugar?

FRANK *shakes his head.*

Jack, Social Services.

JACK (*reads*). 'In response to recommendations from the relevant inspectorate, we have already begun the process of downsizing children's home provision and shifting those resources to "preventive care".'

GEORGE (*interrupts*). Barry, your welcome nod.

BARRY. We have received an intimation that our bid for a Single Regeneration Budget grant has been won by Broughton Moor.

JACK (*to* ALEX). Confirming it's as much of a disaster area as you were confident that it would prove to be.

BARRY. And it looks like we'll get EU money specifically for Back Moor Lane.

GEORGE. So the good news is, we can rescue your fallen women. Thanks of course to Councillor Rafique.

ALEX. And the bad news?

GEORGE *nods to* ANWAR, *who takes a jiffy bag to* ALEX.

ANWAR. Sadly, I fear free condoms are not quite such a popular idea among my electorate in Broughton Moor.

He hands ALEX *the jiffy bag. She looks inside.*

ALEX. I see.

ALEX *shares a look with* RIAZ.

JACK. And naturally, whatever the EU comes up with, we have to match their contribution.

DEREK. Just like with all the rest.

GEORGE *sits. Consulting his notes:*

GEORGE. 'The rest' including, as it happens, a non-faith-specific annual winter Festival, held to mark Eid, Diwali and subsequently Christmas. A multifaith ceremony to mark Holocaust Day was proposed by Councillor Goldman and seconded by Councillor Rafique. A plan for a Festival of Faiths to mark St George's Day – emphasising the diverse and multicultural nature of modern Wyverdale – were proposed by Councillor Rafique – again – seconded by me and passed by acclamation.

GEORGE *thinks he's finished but he hasn't.* BARRY INGS *nods towards* ANWAR HAFIZ.

Oh, ay. In which spirit, a new post of Cabinet Member for Equalities will be filled by Councillor Hafiz, whose first goal will be to review our priorities on grants to voluntary bodies. And then to oversee a new translation service, tasked with ensuring that henceforward all Council leaflets, notices and such will be produced in Punjabi, Mirpuri, Pushtu, Urdu and Bengali.

ARTHUR. To pay for all of which, the following widows and orphans will be flung into the snow . . .

GEORGE. And while it's unrealistic to anticipate an immediate improvement in the representativeness of the Council workforce, we have taken a stepchanging role in establishing best practice in this field by making further changes at the top.

Pause. STEPHEN *and* ALEX *don't get this.*

FRANK. By which the Leader means that I've just been fired.

GEORGE. No, Frank, you've not been fired.

FRANK. I have graciously acceded to a non-negotiable proposal that I resign as Cabinet Member for Education.

GEORGE. And take on / the important –

FRANK. I believe I'm chairing Police Liaison.

ALEX. And so, who . . .

GEORGE. Councillor Rafique has accepted the portfolio of Cabinet Member for Lifelong Learning.

RIAZ *gestures a slightly desperate shrug.*

ALEX. I see.

JACK. I'm sorry, Alex, is there a problem?

ALEX. No.

GEORGE. Obviously these are interim proposals and there's much else to do. For instance, we accept the need to rigorously challenge given notions as to the most appropriate forms of service delivery. But, all in all . . .

STEPHEN *standing, sorting himself to go.*

STEPHEN. So all in all, there's a lot there to digest. To which both of us look forward eagerly. George, Barry, everyone. Thank you so much.

DEREK. Class dismissed.

STEPHEN *briskly goes to shake* GEORGE*'s hand.*

ARTHUR. So is that it?

STEPHEN. In what sense?

JACK (*stands*). In the sense that we hoped you might come to a conclusion.

STEPHEN. Well . . .

ARTHUR (*stands*). Like if you're going to call off the bloody tanks.

Pause.

STEPHEN. Well, naturally, I have to . . .

JACK. Naturally.

STEPHEN. But it is hard, at this, this moment, to envisage circumstances in which formal intervention would be necessary. In the short term, obviously.

ARTHUR. Right.

He goes out.

GEORGE. Well, then. I declare this meeting closed.

STEPHEN. Barry.

He goes to talk to BARRY INGS.

ALEX. George . . .

GEORGE (*tapping his watch*). Beg pardon.

GEORGE *goes out.* JACK *and* DEREK *smiling, feeling victorious, on their way out.*

ALEX. Uh – group minutes?

DEREK. On their way.

DEREK *and* JACK *go out, followed by* MARJORY. RIAZ RAFIQUE *hangs around, not wanting to be noticed but not wanting to go, as* FRANK *approaches* ALEX.

ALEX. 'To rigorously challenge.'

FRANK. 'To effectively compete.'

ALEX. Look, I obviously didn't –

FRANK. Obviously. But we must always consider the consequences of our actions.

Slight pause.

ALEX. Uh, I . . .

BARRY INGS *goes out.* STEPHEN *approaches* ALEX. RIAZ *is feeling increasingly isolated and uncomfortable.*

FRANK. And you know, when we have a group of youngsters declaring this district or that park a no-go area to another group of youngsters, you might think that expenditure on festivals is something of a luxury. But then . . . no longer my domain.

ALEX. Look, Frank . . .

FRANK. Now, Minister, you'll know this. Four years ago, Alex here was Interim Chief Executive of a major north-east London borough. What I can't quite work out from the cuttings is, why / she –

STEPHEN (*firmly, holding out his hand*). Frank, how good to see you.

FRANK. Now, I take it, that is a dismissal?

STEPHEN *demurs.* FRANK, *to* ALEX:

Fine. Well, at least, for now.

He goes out. Clearly, ALEX *and* STEPHEN *want to speak alone.* RIAZ *decides to go, leaving a file behind. He gives an airy wave to* ALEX *as he goes.*

ALEX. It is deeply suspect, Stephen.

STEPHEN. Now what do you suppose Frank meant by / 'Fine for now – '

ALEX. We haven't seen a word of the small print.

STEPHEN. No, but the large print's looking excellent.

ALEX. They haven't looked at council-tax collection or the wage bill.

STEPHEN. Alex, give them time.

ALEX. Time? Stephen, you have no idea / how long it takes them to –

STEPHEN. They gave you member training, children's residential and / diversity –

ALEX. And the Hovis ad stuff about horny-handed grandfathers before us stretching back yeah generation unto generation.

STEPHEN. What about it?

ALEX. He pressed your buttons, Stephen. And you lit up like the Golden Mile.

STEPHEN *gives a slight shake of his head.*

And sure, they mouthed the words. Remarkably effectively. They clearly still don't know the tune. Or rather, it's still 'Raise the scarlet standard high.'

STEPHEN. Alex, you got a result. Give the guys a break.

ALEX. And as you've just witnessed a clear strategy to drop me in it, I'd view it as a courtesy if you took what I said seriously.

Slight pause.

STEPHEN. Of course I take you seriously.

As RIAZ *enters with a document:*

ALEX. And if as your advisor I decide the time has come to accept the Polish Strategy has tanked and that it's time for the Czechoslovak Option . . .

STEPHEN. Oh, and what / d'you mean –

ALEX. That, on this occasion, you will back me up.

Pause.

STEPHEN. Can I ask exactly what you mean by 'the Czechoslovak Option'? Under current circumstances?

ALEX. Not until you say 'yes'.

Pause.

STEPHEN. Yes.

STEPHEN *sees* RIAZ.

We'll talk tomorrow.

He goes out. ALEX *turns to* RIAZ.

ALEX. Ah. Councillor Rafique.

RIAZ. I didn't know.

ALEX. You could have warned me.

RIAZ. I was called into the meeting.

ALEX. And you couldn't have / come out –

RIAZ. I tried. Your phone was off.

ALEX. Of course my phone was off. I was in – a meeting.

Something's wrong with ALEX*'s eye.*

Shit.

She sits at the table, going through her bag.

RIAZ. What's the matter?

ALEX. Contact lens. When I get worked up . . . it goes . . .

She's found a mirror and a tissue. She is taking out her contact lens.

RIAZ. Goes . . . ?

ALEX. You don't want to know.

RIAZ. My uncle is an oculist.

ALEX. My uncle's a solicitor. But I assure you, you wouldn't want me conveyencing your house.

RIAZ. I'm a solicitor. I wouldn't need you to.

ALEX (*putting on a pair of glasses*). Yes, I know that. But the point –

RIAZ. But hey . . . You're beautiful.

ALEX takes a moment to get that this is an upending of the movie cliché of the librarian taking off her glasses.

ALEX. And a respectable wife, and mother.

RIAZ. Ah, I misunderstood.

ALEX. Which bit?

RIAZ. It doesn't matter.

ALEX. All right. An amicably separated wife and mother.

RIAZ. I too . . .

ALEX. Yes, I know. And not just separated.

RIAZ. In my religion we believe we are . . . just separated.

ALEX. And in mine. Um, not that I . . .

RIAZ. But even so, it is hard to move from anger to acceptance.

ALEX. Yes, of course.

Picking up there's something else.

Uh, why?

RIAZ. The circumstances of her death.

ALEX. Uh, do you want / to talk –

RIAZ. Which were that she died giving birth. Or rather, she contracted an infection, which caused her to die.

ALEX. And this was – Wyverdale Infirmary?

RIAZ. No, the Red Crescent Hospital, Dacca. On a visit home.

Pause.

ALEX. Your wife was born in Bangladesh?

RIAZ. Born and raised.

ALEX. So it was . . . you met her there?

RIAZ. Well, her family knew my family.

ALEX. So your marriage was – arranged?

RIAZ. Well, it was planned.

ALEX. I meant –

RIAZ. Otherwise the guests go hungry.

ALEX. No, I meant –

RIAZ. But if your question is, do her parents like me? . . .

ALEX. No, it isn't. But I'm sure they do.

RIAZ. In fact, they asked me if they might bring up our
daughter.

ALEX. So, who . . . ?

RIAZ. My mother.

ALEX. Yes, me too. Well, as we speak.

RIAZ. And there is no, current . . .

ALEX. There is. But he lives in Sweden. Well, kind of.

RIAZ. Kind of Sweden?

ALEX. Kind of – is.

Pause.

RIAZ. I see.

ALEX. But . . . even so.

Pause. To change the subject:

So is that group minutes?

RIAZ. Yes.

He hands the document over.

ALEX (*flipping*). I still can't believe he fired Frank Wilkins.

RIAZ. So who should he have / fired?

ALEX. Well, obviously, Jack Ross.

RIAZ. Oh, why?

ALEX *is finding oddities in the document.*

ALEX. Well, one, because he has been consistently obstructive to recovery. And, two, he has a criminal conviction for a sex offence.

RIAZ. Not everybody sees it as a sex offence.

ALEX. Oh, don't they?

RIAZ. And of course it is no longer criminal.

ALEX. What isn't?

RIAZ. What he was convicted for.

ALEX. Since when?

RIAZ. Since they dropped the legal age from 21 down to 18.

Pause.

ALEX. It was a boy.

RIAZ. A 'boy' of 19. In a club. What did you think it was?

ALEX *works this out. To cover her anger at herself, she goes and takes the jiffy bag of condoms from the table and drops them in a wastepaper basket. Then:*

ALEX. Someone might have fucking told me.

RIAZ. I didn't know you knew.

ALEX. It seems I didn't know.

RIAZ. Well, quite.

ALEX (*waving the minutes*). And while we're on selective information, may I ask why this is printed every other page?

RIAZ. There was a problem with Derek's laptop and the Finance department printer.

ALEX. And the hamster ate his homework.

RIAZ. But I have spent the evening trying to persuade twenty-seven Labour die-hards to buy into performance indicators, market-testing services and closing children's homes, in part on your behalf, and if I haven't quite succeeded, I apologise.

ALEX. Look, I'm not saying . . .

Her phone goes.

Just hang on.

RIAZ. I better go.

ALEX. No, *don't*.

Seeing who the call's from.

Oh, damn.

She answers the phone.

(*Phone.*) Hi, sweetheart.

RIAZ. See you.

ALEX. Riaz . . .

He goes out. ALEX *on the phone:*

No, lovely. So, how's Granny?

Well, it sounds like it's the batteries. I'm sure that Granny . . .

As she speaks, she sits and continues to flip through the minutes.

Jake, please don't be difficult. They're just the same as normal crisps. It's just they're Mexican. I'm sure that Granny thought . . .

Glance at watch.

And now isn't it . . .

OK. I love you too. Give Granny a big special jumbo four-star turbo-powered sloppy one from me.

She ends the call, sits for a moment, checks a page of the minutes and immediately dials again.

Hi, Stephen, Alex. I'm going to have someone email you the small print. It's possible you'll just get the odd pages but even so, I would direct you to page five para 14.b. I think it's, next stop Prague.

STEPHEN CROFT *enters and speaks out front as* ALEX *stands and goes out and the scene changes.*

STEPHEN. Do you remember what they used to say? Football: a game in which two teams kick a ball around a pitch for ninety minutes and the Germans win. Well, that was politics. Two parties kick each other for three weeks every four years and she gets back in. And, OK, so we may not have done everything. One day, who knows, we may even lose. But we must still hang on to why we lost so many times before. The cause, and how it was addresseed.

Holds up his mobile phone.

So I told her, yeah, sure, I was taken in. So, whatever button she wants pressing now, I'll press it.

He goes out.

Scene Eight

For the first time, suddenly, we are in the countryside, high up on the moors. A bright, clean, clear November day. RIAZ RAFIQUE walks in from his car, carrying a towel. He is well wrapped up. ALEX runs on, stops, looks at her stopwatch, bends over and breathes heavily.

RIAZ (*athletics commentator*). A new course, county, national, / commonwealth . . .

ALEX. Shit. You scared the living daylights out of me.

RIAZ. I'm sorry.

ALEX. How on earth did you . . . ?

RIAZ. I went to your hotel. Apparently, they marked you up a map. They marked one up for me.

ALEX. You know what happens to blokes who pick up girls in cars.

RIAZ. Or scantily clad women standing on street corners.

ALEX. But luckily, no CCTV.

RIAZ. I wouldn't put it past them.

ALEX. How can I be sweating. It's so cold.

RIAZ *hands her the towel, which she uses.*

So, may I ask . . . ?

RIAZ. I wanted to apologise.

ALEX. *You* wanted to apologise?

RIAZ. And to ask you, what's the Czechoslovak Option?

ALEX. It's what's not the Polish Strategy or the Indochina Syndrome.

RIAZ. Well, that's cleared that up.

ALEX. It's what we'll have to do if the Cabinet continues to obstruct the necessary programme for the town's recovery.

RIAZ. Oh, you think we're doing that?

ALEX. Yes, since I read the plans for 'discouraging' outsiders tendering for Council contracts.

RIAZ. And the Polish Strategy?

ALEX. Is when you persuade the existing government to do what you want doing. Which clearly isn't going to happen.

RIAZ. Whereas . . .

ALEX. Whereas the Czechoslovak Option is when you identify a leader who you think can run the country properly and you find a means to get him into power. In the Czech case, by sending in the tanks. In our case, by exploitation of a loophole in Chapter 22 of the Local Government Act 2000.

Pause.

RIAZ. Which . . . ?

ALEX. Which allows the Secretary of State to instruct an authority to hold a referendum on the direct election of a mayor. Who could outflank the real problem – which is of course the twenty-seven die-hards on the Labour Group – and put someone in full executive authority who actually believes in the recovery.

RIAZ. You don't think they believe in it?

ALEX. What, Jack Ross closing children's homes?

RIAZ. They've accepted market testing.

ALEX. No, they haven't. According to the / minutes –

RIAZ. But you don't think, given time, / that they –

ALEX. Oh, 'time'. And if I just 'understood the politics'. Well, no. I don't think 'given time'. And actually, you know . . .

RIAZ. Uh, when you say, 'identify a leader who you think can run the country properly' . . . ?

She says nothing. He gets what she's suggesting.

Are you suggesting Wyverdale is ready for a Bangladeshi mayor? Are you suggesting that the *Labour Party's* / ready . . .

ALEX. I am suggesting Wyverdale is crying out for a leader who can find the website of the European Social Fund. And if you can persuade the twenty-seven die-hards to agree to member training, you can persuade the District Party to select a candidate who both believes in the recovery and can deliver it.

RIAZ. And if I don't persuade them?

ALEX. You do a Ken. Stand as an independent. Make your case directly to the people. Because, you see . . .

Slight pause.

I'm not sure it's enough, that they believe it. I'm not sure they'll deliver, even then.

Slight pause.

RIAZ. You know what they say, 'a monkey in a red rosette . . . '

ALEX. But now there's an alternative.

RIAZ. And I was going to . . .

ALEX. Yes, what?

RIAZ. You haven't noticed, that's your towel.

She looks at the towel.

ALEX. So, how . . . ?

RIAZ. I checked you out.

ALEX. You 'checked me out'?

RIAZ. I said I was your chauffeur.

ALEX. You checked me out of my hotel?

RIAZ. I even paid the extras. What's with you and Pringles?

ALEX. Oh, and what exactly do you have in mind with regard to my / accommodation?

RIAZ. My cousin runs a restaurant in Whitby. It's got a flat above which overlooks the bay. It's where Count Dracula lands in the book.

ALEX. But, where . . . ?

RIAZ. They're in Sylhet for the winter. I have the keys. I check it out from time to time.

ALEX. Uh, Riaz . . .

RIAZ. There are several bedrooms.

ALEX. That's all right then.

RIAZ. Or I could drive you back to Wyverdale.

A moment.

ALEX. Barry Ings was setting up a meeting with what they're optimistically calling the Director of Performance.

RIAZ. But, even so.

Pause. They look at each other.

ALEX. I'm freezing. I presume you packed a kind of faded purple woolly?

RIAZ. I would call it violet. So, do you want to come to / Whitby?

ALEX. There's a game where you have to guess what made the other person fall for you. Which of course is never what it is.

Slight pause.

So, in my case, I'd assume it was when I showed such dazzling chutzpah dealing with the tarts on Back Moor Lane.

RIAZ. But that *is* what made me fall for you.

ALEX. Well, that makes it a short round.

RIAZ. And I assume – that, um . . . it would be, something similar. That's if you, actually . . .

RIAZ *is about to say something.* ALEX *puts her finger on his lips.*

Get my pullover before I die.

RIAZ goes to his car. Alone, ALEX *gets out her phone and makes a call.*

ALEX (*phone*). Hallo, Barry? Alex. I just wondered . . .

Oh. Uh – when was this?

Yes, sure. No, understood. On Monday.

RIAZ returns with ALEX's *pullover.*

RIAZ. Look, Alex, I . . .

She ends the call. He sees her face.

What's happening?

ALEX. It's more, what's happened. You know a Pakistani cab driver was bottled Tuesday night in Thawston?

RIAZ. Typically.

ALEX. Quite.

RIAZ. So, what . . . ?

ALEX. At three o'clock this morning, Darren Somebody was seen in conversation with a white girl on Back Moor Lane, and was attacked by Asian vigilantes who assumed she was a tart and he was a punter or a pusher or a pimp. An altercation then ensued in which remarks were made of a racially abusive character and knives were drawn. Then Darren was rushed to hospital, and they declared him dead an hour ago. As the *Clarion* reporter put it when he called up Barry, in this case, the tit does seem to trump the tat.

She puts on her pullover.

What's happening, Riaz? Have I missed something? What is happening here?

RIAZ. Do you mean, here Wyverdale? Or, here here?

Pause.

ALEX. Of course, it was when you told me all about your father's secret store of English mustard, on my voicemail.

Slight pause.

And you know that if a whisper of this got out . . .

Slight pause.

How far is Whitby?

Scene Nine

Wyverdale cenotaph. The Holocaust Commemoration, 27 January the following year. STEPHEN, GEORGE, FRANK, DEREK, JACK, ARTHUR, RIAZ, ANWAR, YUSUF, *the* MAYOR, LES SLATER, SHIRLEY HONEYWELL, *a* BRITANNIA SUPPORTER, KURSHID HAFIZ, MICHELE *from the manicurists', other* TOWNSPEOPLE. SUPERINTENDANT RICKS *is in attendance* (*along with other* POLICE), *as is a white* SCHOOLGIRL, *an Asian* SCHOOLBOY, *an* ASIAN WOMAN *in a wheelchair and the* BISHOP. *It is possible a school orchestra plays the theme from* Schindler's List.

STEPHEN (*out front*). And the 27th of January is a cold and misty Friday and as usual I am driving up to my constituency and I decide it would be politic – and right – to break my journey.

ARTHUR (*out front*). Friday afternoon. Grand time for a three-line whip.

MAYOR (*reading from notes, not very well*). Ladies and Gentlemen, this is a most important day for every citizen of Wyverdale, especially the young folks, in that today we must remember past events, in view of making doubly sure it won't ever be repeated in the future.

JACK (*out front*). And stones are laid and seven candles lit.

DEREK (*out front*). One for each million and one for all the others.

ANWAR (*out front*). And there are verses from the Bible and the Torah and the Koran.

DEREK (*out front*). And as ever Pastor Niemoeller is wheeled out for the occasion.

Pause. Everyone looks at the MAYOR.

(*Out front.*) And, as ever . . .

MAYOR. Oh, beg pardon.

She reads:

First they came for the – communists but I did not speak out. Because I was not a communist.

BISHOP. Then they came for the trade unionists and I did not speak out because I was not a trade unionist.

ASIAN WOMAN. Then they came for the lesbians and gays and the disabled.

SCHOOLBOY. Then they came for the Jews and I was not a Jew . . .

SCHOOLGIRL. And then they came for me. And there was no one left to speak on my behalf.

ALEX *enters, nodding apologetically.*

STEPHEN (*out front*). And then suddenly, like a twenty-five to one outsider on the blind side, it began to happen.

LES SLATER *has taken a wreath to the cenotaph.*
SHIRLEY *follows him.*

LES. Good afternoon. This is a cenotaph.

BISHOP. Um . . .

LES. All sorts, you can do here. Sing songs, read poetry, light candles. Call to prayer. But the thing it's for is laying wreaths.

He shows the wreath to both sides.

This is a wreath. This is what you say. This is in remembrance of all genocides and holocausts, everywhere in the world, including against white people in places like Zimbabwe and maybe not too far from here and all.

He nods to SHIRLEY, *who opens a piece of paper and begins to read the words to 'I Vow to Thee, My Country'.*

SHIRLEY.
I vow to thee, my country,
All earthly things above,
Entire and whole and perfect,
The service of my love.

DEREK. No, I'm sorry, I'm not having this.

DEREK *goes and grabs the wreath and starts to rip it up. As he does so the inscription falls to the ground.*

This is Les Slater of Britannia, a racist party. They believe in genocide. Their leaders think the Holocaust din't happen.

LES *holds up the inscription.*

LES. This is the inscription on the wreath. 'In memory of Darren Purdy, 20 years of age. Murdered by Islamic fundamentalists on November 11th – '

DEREK *goes for* LES – SHIRLEY *attacks* DEREK *from behind.*

JACK. Eh, come on, Derek –

GEORGE (*to* SHIRLEY). Get off him, love –

LES *has broken free from* DEREK, *grabbed* MICHELE'*s hand, and holds it up.*

LES. This is Darren's mother. This is Michele Purdy. She's just seen her son's wreath torn up / in front of her –

DEREK *attacks* LES.

DEREK. No, look, cunt.

SHIRLEY. That's charming, that is.

LES. Belt her, go on, lay one on her.

RICKS *intervenes to pull* DEREK *off.*

RICKS. Now, come on, lad –

DEREK. I'm not a lad, I'm a fucking councillor.

The melee increases. As it does so, FRANK WILKINS *goes to the cenotaph, picks up the wreath, and taps the microphone.*

KURSHID. This is lies. He weren't murdered.

DEREK. Get *off* me.

RICKS. Calm down.

DEREK. No way.

SHIRLEY. This is democracy! This is democracy in Wyverdale!

KURSHID. We all know what he were doing there.

FRANK. Please. Please, everybody. It's important that you understand.

The fighting slowly subsides.

KURSHID (*to* ANWAR). Who's this?

FRANK. He's right. It is surely crucial everybody knows that the person who ripped up this wreath is a member of your Labour Council.

DEREK. Oh, fuck off, Frank.

GEORGE. Frank?

FRANK. You might ask, what kind of group of people this might be, so careless of a mother's grief.

JACK goes and tries to take the microphone.

JACK. Frank, stop this.

FRANK (*pulling the microphone towards him to keep it from JACK*). But of course – it is quite typical.

By now everyone is listening.

A body so concerned with its own political survival. That will discriminate in the name of non-discrimination.

MAYOR (*to GEORGE*). What's going off?

FRANK. Organisations that have been given grants by your Council since November. The Pakistani Welfare Group. Broughton Against Racism. The Islamic this, Kashmiri that.

JACK. Frank, leave it out.

FRANK. And the translation unit. Hands up how many people here need, genuinely need, their council-tax-collection leaflet translated into Pushtu? Enough to warrant the suspension of the traffic-calming programme in West Thawston? Or the closure of two swimming baths? But of course, they're not in Broughton Moor. So they don't get special money from the Government.

MAYOR. Is this supposed to happen?

GEORGE. No, Maureen.

BISHOP. Um, Councillor . . .

FRANK. I cannot in all conscience carry on as a member of the Labour Group. I owe it to the decent ordinary folk of Wyverdale who voted for me, to resign the Labour whip and sit henceforward as an independent.

GEORGE. Frank, you've said your piece . . .

FRANK. And if they say, as say they will, 'Well, this is all
fine, but we're nearly bankrupt and we've got Whitehall on
our backs and our hands are tied and there's nothing we can
do,' just ask them why there's no asylum-seekers left in
Wyverdale. And if they're honest they'll admit it's because
George Aldred did a deal to stop them coming here.

He holds up the wreath.

So if they say there's nothing they can do . . . Imagine.

He leaves the microphone. Applause and booing.

GEORGE. Frank, what you playing at?

LES. Well, that's told 'em!

SHIRLEY. Gonna join us?

FRANK *passes* GEORGE *and* ALEX.

JACK. Good fucking question.

FRANK. I hold Britannia in even more contempt than I hold
you.

SHIRLEY. Oh, ay.

LES. Leave 'em be.

LES *and* SHIRLEY *go.*

FRANK (*to* ALEX). Something that might be of interest. The
girl Darren Purdy was protecting. Apparently until October,
she lived at number 37 Bellevue Crescent, Thawston. Which
was a children's home. Until you made us close it.

ALEX. What?

GEORGE. Frank, what you bloody playing at?

FRANK. The 42nd verse, the 21st chapter, the Gospel
according to St Matthew.

FRANK *hands* ALEX *the broken wreath and goes out.*

GEORGE (*to* STEPHEN). Not just children's homes and all.

STEPHEN. Hallo, George.

GEORGE. Even so, your mayoral referendum. Postals coming
in at two to one in favour.

STEPHEN. It's not 'my' referendum.

GEORGE. But you want it passing.

ARTHUR. Get a True Believer into place.

STEPHEN. I want what's best for Wyverdale.

ARTHUR (*turning to* ALEX). Eh, don't you fret, love. You can still make the 16.20 via Wakefield.

ARTHUR *and* GEORGE *go out.* STEPHEN *throws a look to* ALEX *then follows. The stage is almost empty.* ALEX *turns to* RIAZ. MICHELE *is watching them.*

ALEX. The Indochina Syndrome. It's when you do what you think is the right thing, and you get sucked in and then it turns on you and everything you do to try to extracate yourself just makes it worse. Which is why – right now – I'd like to be in your car headed back to Whitby.

RIAZ. Alex, Darren Purdy was killed in my ward.

ALEX. Of course. A time like this. But even so.

RIAZ *goes out.* MICHELE *comes over to* ALEX.

MICHELE. I know you.

ALEX. Yes. You did my nails and told me all about the Pakis.

MICHELE *and* ALEX *look at each other.* MICHELE *turns and goes.* ALEX *is left, standing, holding the wreath in her hands.*

End of Act One.

'How can we ensure that people feel a sense of pride in being British — without feeling that they have to leave other traditions behind?

How can we ensure that pride in being British is combined with respect for other people's identities?

What role can shared values play in this?

In what way can we promote British citizenship for all, particularly among young people?

How can we ensure that all communities see racist, racial and religious harassment and hate crimes as unacceptable and are able to act to drive them out?

How can we most effectively respond to the threat from political and other forms of extremism, including understanding and tackling its causes?

How can we effectively target policies to tackle the specific disadvantages experienced by sections of the population within a strategy that delivers equality for all?

What more can we do to build relationships and understanding between people from all backgrounds?'

Diversity Consultation,
Home Office, 2004

ACT TWO

Scene One

Nine months later. A room in the Oddfellows Hall, Wyverdale, which has been set up for a Public Inquiry. There is a table behind which sits the Inquiry Chair, BOB STANLEY, who is in his 50s, and the Inquiry counsel, JILL WATTS, who is around 40. At a smaller table RANJIT SINGH KHERA, 33, acting for Broughton Families for Peace. There is a single chair for WITNESSES, a couple of chairs for WITNESSES awaiting their turn, and a chair and small desk for the TRANSCRIBER. There is an USHER who sits to the side, and a section of the room for PRESS and PUBLIC. There may be screens on which documents can be displayed, video footage played, or the faces of WITNESSES shown.

The feel, structure and groundrules of the dramatisation follow those of the tribunal plays at the Tricycle Theatre in London. (Though in this case the physical set-up is less formal, as the Inquiry is not judicial.) During the evidence, people come and go. The TRANSCRIBERS work in shifts and change over from time to time. The presentation of the Inquiry is continuous in dramatic action but is clearly compressed – so while some WITNESS presentations are topped and tailed, others (we imagine) begin in the middle, or continue after the section we've chosen to dramatise. Similarly, we assume that the different COUNSEL introduce themselves to each WITNESS, but after the first time, this introduction is only represented when dramatically significant. On occasions it is important that we see WITNESSES sit down in the waiting area at a particular point, and that certain people are present in the public area, in which case it's specified.

At the beginning, the COUNSEL and TRANSCRIBER are waiting. The first witness, MICHAEL FARRELL, is in the waiting area. The public area is reasonably full.

USHER. Ladies and gentlemen, could you please switch off all pagers, bleepers and . . .

A mobile phone goes off in the public area.

. . . mobile phones.

The phone is hurriedly switched off. BOB STANLEY *comes in. Some* PEOPLE *stand – though not the* COUNSEL. *As* STANLEY *takes off his jacket, puts it on the back of his chair, and sits at his table:*

STANLEY. No, no.

PEOPLE *sit.*

Good morning. Today we start with . . .

WATTS. Michael Farrell.

STANLEY. Mr Farrell, my name is Bob Stanley, and I'm a member of the House of Lords, and I'm Chair of this Inquiry.

MICHAEL. Right.

STANLEY. And this is Mrs Watts, who is Counsel for the Inquiry and will be asking you some questions.

MICHAEL. Fine.

STANLEY. I think – the microphones are sensitive, there isn't any need to lean into them to speak.

MICHAEL *leans back.*

WATTS. Mr Farrell, what's your job?

MICHAEL. I work as a waiter at the George Hotel.

WATTS. And where do you live?

MICHAEL. In Fenleydale.

WATTS. Which is a suburb, north of central Wyverdale. Can you describe your journey to work on the 23rd of April?

MICHAEL. Well, I got the Number 16 bus round half past four.

WATTS. You were on the evening shift?

MICHAEL. That's right.

WATTS. And what's the route of your journey on the Number 16?

STANLEY. There is a street map on your screens.

MICHAEL. The bus normally goes from Fenley High Street down the Thawston Road then through Broughton Moor, down Back Moor Lane, which bears left into North Street and then Northgate where the George is.

WATTS. But on this day, as I understand it, the bus stopped before it got to North Street, for, what, ten minutes?

MICHAEL. While I got off.

WATTS. And what did you assume had happened?

MICHAEL. Beg pardon?

WATTS. I assume a traffic jam wasn't normal on a Sunday.

MICHAEL. Well, on this particular Sunday there were going to be a parade, like. For the St George. But it were cancelled, but there were people saying, 'We're going to make our protest anyroad.' Now as it happened it weren't that happening but that's what I s'pose I assumed.

WATTS. But when you left the bus you found out what it was.

MICHAEL. Too right.

WATTS. Which was?

MICHAEL. A group of lads throwing bricks and bottles at a pub.

WATTS. How many lads?

MICHAEL. Well, I didn't stop to count, like.

WATTS. Approximately? Double figures?

MICHAEL. Oh, ay. Thirty plus.

WATTS. And what did you do?

MICHAEL. There's a street connects with North Street higher up.

STANLEY. And can I just check, if you can see the street map, that the place the bus stopped was just above the little star marked two.

MICHAEL. Yuh. That's the Admiral Nelson.

WATTS. And, who were the brick and bottle throwers? I mean, in ethnic terms.

MICHAEL. Well, they were Asian, weren't they.

WATTS. Exclusively?

MICHAEL. Oh, ay.

WATTS. Now, you get to the hotel. It's now round, what? Five or five fifteen?

MICHAEL. Ay, round that.

WATTS. Is it busy?

MICHAEL. Well, we'd two functions.

WATTS. One of which I understand was a civic reception connected with the St George Festival?

MICHAEL. Ay.

WATTS. Attended by a large number of councillors, a minister, a visiting celebrity.

MICHAEL. That's right.

WATTS. And the other function?

MICHAEL. Were a themed affair. Wedding anniversary.

STANLEY. When you say 'a themed affair'?

MICHAEL. I mean, a do. With dinner, dancing and a band. And like, a theme.

WATTS. And once at the hotel, you became aware that the disturbances were spreading out of Broughton Moor and into the town centre.

MICHAEL. Yes.

WATTS. And then?

MICHAEL. Well, it were outside, weren't it?

WATTS. That's on Northgate, which contains the frontage of the George.

MICHAEL. That's right.

WATTS. And this was because by now the police had set up a defensive line on Northgate, and what by now we can call the rioters were pressing down on it. Just where the lowest explosion marker is, on the map.

MICHAEL. Number three.

WATTS. And could you see this?

MICHAEL. Only from upstairs. It were more like we could hear. And what people said who came in off the street.

WATTS. So people came in?

MICHAEL. Yes. Until the police locked up the front.

WATTS. And what happened to the people inside the hotel? I mean, the people at the do's, the guests.

MICHAEL. They were subject to an evacuation procedure.

WATTS. And did everybody go?

MICHAEL. Not everybody, no.

STANLEY. Did you go?

MICHAEL. Well, I didn't fancy my chances of like getting home. I mean, by now, they were burning out the pubs and shops and that. And – well.

STANLEY. Well what?

MICHAEL. Well, s'not summat you like get to see every day. A ringside seat, like.

WATTS. Which was?

MICHAEL. Room 307.

WATTS. And in the morning in the daylight there were scenes of devastation.

MICHAEL. We didn't get ourselves reopened while the Wednesday after.

WATTS. Thank you.

STANLEY. Mr Farrell, I'll be asking everyone three questions. What they think started the violence. What were the deeper causes. And the effect that these events have had on Wyverdale.

Pause.

MICHAEL. See, we used to be a place'd sometimes get to the semifinals of the FA Cup. Now, I mean, like for a laugh like, we pick up the phone and say, 'Good evening, Beirut Hilton.'

STANLEY. Thank you very much.

SUPERINTENDANT BERNARD RICKS *takes over the stand.* SHIRLEY *in the public area.*

Mr Ricks, I am the Chair of the Inquiry. This is Mrs Watts, who is asking questions on behalf of the Inquiry.

Pause.

RICKS. Fine. In fact, I should say / at the outset that I was –

STANLEY. I should say that as we don't have power to subpoena witnesses we're very grateful for your agreeing to give evidence.

RICKS. Yes, well, it wasn't entirely my decision.

STANLEY. But even so.

WATTS. Can you please tell us who you are?

RICKS. I am Superintendant Bernard Ricks.

WATTS. And you are the senior police officer for the central division of Wyverdale?

RICKS. That's right.

STANLEY. I should say that in the interests of informality, we have agreed to dispense with official titles, so Mrs Watts will call you Mr Ricks.

RICKS. As you did.

STANLEY. Yes.

WATTS. Mr Ricks, I want to take you back to Saturday the 22nd April, the day before the riot. I want to ask you about the decision to ban both the threatened march by members of an extremist organisation and a parade planned as a centrepiece for the Festival of Faiths.

RICKS. I have to say that wasn't my decision.

WATTS. But you supported it?

RICKS. I recommended it.

WATTS. Can you remind us of the nature of those two events?

RICKS. Well, the Festival of Faiths was an event organised by the Town Council to be held on St George's Day.

WATTS. With what purpose?

RICKS. Well, St George is patron saint of England.

WATTS. But that wasn't the sole purpose, surely.

RICKS. I believe the festival was intended to celebrate the diversity of Wyverdale.

WATTS. While the other march, the one announced by Britannia, was intended to proceed from the Morrison estate in Thawston to the town centre. And was not intended to celebrate the diversity of Wyverdale.

RICKS. Well, I don't know that.

WATTS. Britannia is a right-wing, racist body.

RICKS. It's a political party. I believe it has a member on the Council.

SHIRLEY. Two members!

STANLEY *shakes his head to* SHIRLEY.

WATTS. I think that happened subsequent to these events, at the May elections.

RICKS. Well, if you say so.

WATTS. And you received the information about this march plan on the morning of the Saturday.

RICKS. Yes. The march was scheduled for the Sunday.

WATTS. One day later?

RICKS. Yes.

WATTS. While the Festival of Faiths had been announced in, I think, November and had been planned for many months?

RICKS. Yes.

WATTS. Yet you felt the need to ban that as well.

RICKS. No, we didn't ban the festival, which took place across the town as planned. We banned a march which was one item of the festival.

WATTS. So doesn't your decision look like this? There's this march – well, really, a parade – which has been planned for months, as the cornerstone of an event set up to celebrate the town as a community, and now within twenty-four hours of it happening, a group with a clearly divisive political agenda –

SHIRLEY. Shame!

STANLEY. Now, please.

WATTS. This group announces that *they're* going to march, we'll ban them both, it's only fair.

RICKS. I understand what you're implying.

WATTS. Oh, what's that?

RICKS. You're implying that I'm saying these two marches were equivalent. But I assure you, that was not the issue on our minds. The issue was a matter of the risks that either march might pose to the public at a time of heightened tension.

WATTS. All right. I'd like to move on to the events of Sunday afternoon. When did your officers arrive outside the Admiral Nelson?

RICKS. As I recall at approximately five to five.

WATTS. To find what?

RICKS. As it was reported to me, a group of young Asian males attacking the pub with bricks and bottles and other missiles.

WATTS. Do you know how this fracas started?

RICKS. By the time my men arrived, the 'fracas' had already started.

WATTS. At which a number of arrests were made.

RICKS. Correct.

During the following SERGEANT DONALD BAXTER *enters and is directed by the* USHER *to the witness waiting area.*

WATTS. Whereupon the crowd moved from the pub and its environs to the local police station.

RICKS. I wasn't there myself of course.

WATTS. You were at the town-centre station. Where, by now, the arrested people had been moved.

RICKS. Correct.

WATTS. Do you think that was a good decision?

RICKS. It was a very good decision. The Broughton Moor station was surrounded by a mob.

WATTS. Even with what subsequently happened?

RICKS. I'd need to know what you're referring to.

WATTS. I mean, the decision of a substantial section of the crowd to march into the town centre.

RICKS. Oh, right. Yes, I think that it was still the right decision, despite what subsequently happened.

STANLEY. Mr Ricks, Mr Khera is representing Broughton Families for Peace. I think he has some questions for you.

RICKS. Good morning.

KHERA. Morning. In fact, it's really just one question.

KHERA *waits for an acknowledgement from* RICKS *but doesn't get one, so he goes on.*

It's whether, over recent years, your force has felt under pressure, not to be seen as biased against non-white communities.

RICKS. My police force isn't biased against anyone.

KHERA. You don't feel yourself constrained by what you might call 'political correctness'? And thus less able to fulfill your proper function, fighting crime?

RICKS. I would challenge that.

KHERA. Because I put it to you, that if you felt people didn't understand what you were up against, then the events of 23rd April were a very good way of demonstrating that.

RICKS (*to* STANLEY). Did you say 'Families for Peace'?

KHERA. That's the body which I represent.

RICKS. And these are families of people arrested in connection with the Broughton Moor disturbances?

KHERA. Among others, yes.

RICKS. What happened on the 23rd of April was an explosion of violent and often vicious criminality, most of it against

my officers. To imply that they welcomed or provoked it or
didn't stop it when they could have done is a monstrous
allegation.

Blackout.

Lights on SERGEANT DONALD BAXTER. MICHELE
PURDY *is in the public area. During this,* YUSUF IQBAL
and RIAZ *come into the public area.*

WATTS. You are Sergeant Donald Baxter.

BAXTER. Yes.

WATTS. You are a community police officer attached to
Broughton Moor police station.

BAXTER. Yes.

WATTS. And as such, presumably, you had a sense of the
feelings in the town in the months before the riots?

BAXTER. Hopefully.

WATTS. You were aware of a whole series of incidents that
contributed to growing tensions in the town?

BAXTER. Certainly.

WATTS. For instance, when a group of away football fans
marched through Broughton Moor in October last year,
chanting racist slogans and harassing and abusing passers-
by?

BAXTER. Definitely.

WATTS. Then there was a range of incidents concerned with
taxi drivers, most of whom are, as you know, of Pakistani or
Kashmiri heritage.

BAXTER. Yes.

WATTS. The issue here is not only that taxi drivers are
attacked by passers-by and indeed by their own fares, in
predominantly white areas, but that police assistance is slow
in coming and not very helpful.

BAXTER. I've obviously heard this.

WATTS. There are cases of taxi drivers who report attacks,
who are then prosecuted for not having the right insurance
or a working fire-extinguisher.

BAXTER. Well, a taxi should / have a working –

WATTS. While, as they put it, the attackers are streets away.

BAXTER. Well, I've heard such things but I don't know about that specific / example.

WATTS. And those incidents were exacerbated, were they not, by what happened at the war memorial in January, when various inflammatory points were made, about Asians being privileged by the Council, and so forth?

BAXTER. Well, people thought that, yes.

WATTS. And that's not to mention the threat of a march by a far-right group through the town on the same day as the Festival of Faiths?

BAXTER. Well, sure, but . . .

He changes his mind.

Sure, you could say that as well.

KHERA. Mr Baxter, when did you hear about the trouble on the afternoon of the 23rd of April?

BAXTER. Well, I was off that day, so I didn't know immediately. I would say I received a call around 5.15. And I went straight in to Broughton Moor.

KHERA. I'm sorry, didn't you make a call yourself?

BAXTER. Yes, that's right, I'm sorry. I made a call to Councillor Rafique.

KHERA. Who was one of the councillors for the Broughton ward?

BAXTER. Yes.

KHERA. And you felt might help to calm the situation.

BAXTER. Yes.

KHERA. When you arrived at the station, what did you find there?

BAXTER. An angry crowd.

KHERA. This was outside the station?

BAXTER. Outside and inside.

KHERA. And had Mr Rafique arrived?

BAXTER. He had. He was asking questions at the station desk, on behalf of a number of the Asian men inside the station.

KHERA. Who were demanding that the arrested men be released.

BAXTER. Yes.

KHERA. And the others, am I right? They wished to lodge complaints about what had happened in the aftermath of the fight outside the Admiral Nelson. People were complaining about the way in which the police had acted. Going into people's houses, and so forth.

BAXTER. Yes.

KHERA. And what were they told?

BAXTER. That there was a statutory complaints procedure.

KHERA. Which was?

BAXTER. You fill in a complaints form.

KHERA. And did people do that?

BAXTER. Yes.

KHERA. Immediately?

BAXTER. When I'd photocopied copies of the form.

KHERA. Which took you, how long?

BAXTER. Ten or fifteen minutes.

KHERA. And when you got back to the lobby?

BAXTER. Councillor Rafique was inquiring once again about the issue of the arrested men.

KHERA. And what did you do?

BAXTER. I resolved to find out what I could.

KHERA. And what did you find out?

BAXTER. That the men had been removed from Broughton Moor to the town-centre police station.

KHERA. What, recently?

BAXTER. About an hour before.

KHERA. And this was news to you?

BAXTER. Yes.

KHERA. You mean that nobody had told you?

BAXTER. No.

KHERA. And then Councillor Rafique went outside to report back to the crowd.

BAXTER. Yes.

KHERA. And you went with him?

BAXTER. I wouldn't say exactly with him.

KHERA. And he reported to the crowd about the transfer of the men.

BAXTER. Yes.

KHERA. And what was their reaction?

BAXTER. Well, they weren't best pleased.

KHERA. In fact, they booed Mr Rafique.

BAXTER. You could say they blamed the messenger.

KHERA. Because presumably they felt he'd been made to look a patsy.

BAXTER. Yes. That might have been a view.

KHERA. And what was the consequence of this?

BAXTER. Well, Councillor Rafique had been speaking through a megaphone and this was taken by another man who proposed the crowd march to the centre to demand the arrested men's release.

KHERA. And was this accepted?

BAXTER. Well, they started moving off.

KHERA. And what did you do?

BAXTER. I re-entered the police premises and I informed the senior officer in charge of what had transpired.

KHERA. Thank you, that's all I have.

STANLEY. Thank you so much, / Mr Baxter.

BAXTER. Mr Chairman, can I add a point here?

STANLEY. Yes of course.

BAXTER. It's about Mrs Watt's list of incidents.

STANLEY. Go on.

BAXTER. It's just, I think, it's a bit selective. I mean, for instance, last autumn, when Broughton Park, which is the border between Broughton Moor and Thawston, effectively became a no-go area for whites, with people being harassed and made to feel uncomfortable and forced to leave. And then there's the murder of Darren Purdy . . .

WATTS *makes to rise.*

I've no doubt that'll come up.

STANLEY. Yes, it will.

WATTS *sits down again.*

BAXTER. Which gets mixed up with the prostitution business.

STANLEY. How's that?

BAXTER. Well, in the week before the riot, there were posters went up, commemorating Purdy, and condemning us for failing to arrest a suspect, and so forth. 'Darren Purdy, English Martyr.' And there's a little prefabricated building that's a kind of drop-in welfare centre for women in the vice trade. And the posters were stuck up on that.

STANLEY. So, Mr Baxter, the point you're putting here is this: there was a series of events, over many months, provoked by, or enacted by, both the white and Asian populations, almost on a kind of tit-for-tat basis, and one can understand the feelings of both sides.

BAXTER. Oh, sure. I can understand their feelings. My job, understanding people's feelings. And then there's a riot with five million quids' worth of damage and three pubs torched and a sub-post office and a car dealership are trashed and a family burnt out of their restaurant. And I wonder how, with all the understanding, how we failed to stop it.

STANLEY. Thank you.

BAXTER *leaves the stand.*

WATTS. Now we are overrunning slightly, which creates a problem, in that our next but one witness, Mr Yusuf Iqbal, has a train to catch, and if we go in order he may miss it. Might he jump the queue?

STANLEY. I'm happy with that.

YUSUF IQBAL *takes the witness seat.* MICHELE *goes out. During this,* SHIRLEY *and* FAZAL MANSOOR *are in the public area.* FAZAL *is 23, with a light beard. Also an* ASIAN WOMAN *in a jilbab.*

WATTS. You are Yusuf Iqbal.

YUSUF. That is correct.

WATTS. You are Chairman of the Pakistani Welfare Group.

YUSUF. Yes, and I / am also –

WATTS. You are also Secretary of Islamic Relief.

YUSUF. And I am Governor of Broughton Girls School and representative of Broughton Moor Neighbourhood Association on the Wyverdale Strategic Partnership.

WATTS. In short, you are what is commonly called an elder.

YUSUF. I am certainly more elder than most people here.

WATTS. Now, I'm sure the Neighbourhood Association does many things, but it is particularly known for one thing, am I right?

YUSUF (*to* STANLEY). The Association was created with the express task of ridding Broughton Moor of the evils of the prostitution industry.

WATTS. A problem which the police were unable to address?

YUSUF. Unable or unwilling.

WATTS. So you took the matter into your own hands.

YUSUF (*to* STANLEY). We set up patrols, yes.

WATTS. And what would happen if your patrols came across a prostitute?

YUSUF. We hope the presence of concerned residents will discourage them.

WATTS. And if it didn't?

YUSUF (*to* STANLEY). I must make clear, it was not the policy of the Association to use violence.

WATTS. Now, there was a little drop-in centre, providing advice for women on benefits and health and so on. Why did you object to this?

YUSUF. It was a big pat on the back for the prostitution industry.

WATTS. But didn't it provide / advice on how girls might –

YUSUF (*to* STANLEY). Also it was a fine haunt for the drugs trade.

WATTS. Which is a big concern for you?

YUSUF. Well, I would not say, particularly.

WATTS. No? With your young men, with your young women? You must want to protect them, from the less savoury aspects of contemporary British life. And the patrols might be a part of that.

YUSUF. You mean, we might want to protect our children from vomiting and fighting? Or to live in houses where the only printed matter is the Littlewoods catalogue?

WATTS. As I say, from contemporary British culture.

STANLEY. Mrs Watts, I'm not sure where you're headed here.

WATTS. Well, I'm addressing the question of the segregation of Wyverdale's non-white communities. I'm leading up to asking Mr Iqbal, whether he agrees with the common argument, that when the rioters attacked pubs and post offices and car showrooms that it was for a purpose.

YUSUF (*to* STANLEY). Meanwhile white rioters in Thawston burn down a Bangladeshi restaurant.

WATTS. Which is why I put to you the view that the aim of attacking these particular non-Muslim businesses was to drive them out.

FAZAL. Shame!

YUSUF. I cannot speak for what the rioters might do. Which is why we collaborated naturally with the police.

KHERA. Mr Iqbal, when you say 'collaboration with the police', you mean, by encouraging young men to give themselves up?

YUSUF. Yes.

KHERA. By putting pictures up from CCTV footage in the mosque so young men could be identified?

FAZAL (*from the public area*). Shame!

YUSUF. Yes.

KHERA. And parents escorting young men to the police, when they'd been taped committing crimes?

YUSUF. Yes.

FAZAL (*from the public area*). Traitor!

ASIAN WOMAN. Shame!

STANLEY. Now, please.

YUSUF. Because these hotheads had brought shame upon themselves and their community. We deal with shameful circumstances here.

Slight pause.

Some young men were going to get married. Some were studying for HND. My cousin's son was two weeks from his Duke of Edinburgh's Award.

STANLEY. Thank you, Mr / Iqbal –

FAZAL (*not shouted, but audible*). Plonker.

YUSUF. You know, Lord Stanley, that despite all the talk of self-segregation and apartheid and parallel communities, there is a place in Wyverdale where young Asian and young white men work together across ethnic divisions in circumstances of mutual respect and harmony.

STANLEY. And where's that?

YUSUF. The drugs trade. Suppliers, clients, all in perfect harmony together. And it is of course the druggies and the drifters who come back to Islam, switch on their computers, find the websites, and talk of holy war.

Blackout.

The USHER *takes* FAZAL*'s arm.*

USHER. Now come on.

STANLEY. Look, I appreciate this is a matter / that raises high emotions . . .

FAZAL (*pulling his arm away*). The brothers are in Armley Prison for nowt but defending their community.

SHIRLEY. And throwing petrol bombs.

STANLEY. . . . but if you continue, I will have to / stop.

FAZAL. For the Muslim youth of Broughton, self-defence is no offence.

SHIRLEY. So does she get a word in?

FAZAL. Like the things she talks about.

MICHELE. / Don't look like it.

STANLEY. I shall rise for five minutes.

He turns his swivel chair around. WATTS *comes over to him, and they talk, their backs to the rest.*

FAZAL. Them things you said, weren't took off you, you gave 'em up. You give your kids to the drugs and prostitution anyway, and you blame us.

USHER. The session is suspended / for five minutes.

LES (*to* SHIRLEY). Let's go.

FAZAL. And who says as we want social work and handings out and that. Broughton Moor in't no begging bowl.

USHER. / We are in recess.

He goes out, as:

FAZAL. We just want like we're left alone.

SHIRLEY. Oh, that's great, / that is.

FAZAL. And they gives us grants and that to go and live in Fenleydale and Thawston and like integrate. And then what happens anyway?

LES (*to* MICHELE). Come on –

MICHELE. No, no. He's right.

This surprises everyone.

FAZAL. Oh, yeah?

MICHELE. No, you're right an' all, things weren't took off us, we pissed 'em all away, we didn't have to.

FAZAL. Ay, too right.

LES stops SHIRLEY from intervening.

MICHELE. In fact, it's funny, go to Broughton, it's the same like. Just instead of Sunday best for Whitsun it's all Eid and that. And instead of Elsie chattering across the garden fence, s'like Parveen.

FAZAL. Well, yeah, anyway.

MICHELE. So at last we all agree on summat, why not shake on it.

She puts her hand out.

Eh? What say we shake on it?

She holds her hand out.

So go on, Fazal, shake.

She turns to JILL WATTS.

Or if you don't want me, then shake with her. She's closer like to being on your side.

FAZAL. This is a pisstake anyway.

MICHELE (*to* WATTS). Eh. Go on. Shake his hand.

After a moment, JILL WATTS comes forward, puts out her hand to FAZAL. STANLEY turns back and watches. FAZAL doesn't respond.

It's nowt personal. He won't touch women on account of his religion.

To STANLEY:

Well, that's me done.

She sits. A moment. LES and SHIRLEY sit. FAZAL sits. STANLEY decides to go back to his place.

STANLEY. Mrs Purdy, I should say before you go that in other circumstances I would have asked for there to be a minute's silence in memory of Darren.

MICHELE. Oh, ay?

STANLEY. But I must tell you, everybody feels your loss.

MICHELE. You think so? Well.

She sits.

But thanks.

STANLEY. We'll go on to the next witness. Mrs Watts?

ANWAR HAFIZ *stands.*

ANWAR. Mr Chairman, I am Anwar Hafiz.

STANLEY. Yes . . . Councillor Hafiz. We have you scheduled later / as a witness –

ANWAR. I think there is something that's worth saying at this point, however, very briefly.

STANLEY. Well, if it really is / brief.

ANWAR. You ask what began the violence, and what was the deeper cause. And of course the deeper causes are in part what has happened to the places where we live, and our fears for ourselves and for our children, which made us cut those places off, or maybe make them like the places which we left behind. And maybe in that we are a bit like Mrs Purdy.

SHIRLEY (*in the public area*). Hmm!

ANWAR. But there is also what began this riot on this day. Which may be something or somebody very different.

STANLEY. Mr Hafiz, are you saying that you know who started this?

ANWAR. No, I fear I am reporting merely a vile rumour.

SHIRLEY. Someone's nephew telling someone's aunty's cousin.

ANWAR. Yes.

He is about to sit down, when a thought strikes him.

Oh, but one correction. I am not a councillor. I stood down, better to make a bid for higher office.

STANLEY *looks to* WATTS, *questioningly.*

Not, I fear, successfully. But there we are.

Blackout and then lights.

JACK ROSS *in the witness chair.* GEORGE, ARTHUR *and* DEREK *are in the public area, as are* RIAZ *and* ANWAR. *During this,* FRANK WILKINS *comes in, and, after a whispered conversation with the* USHER, *goes to the witness waiting area.*

JACK. My name is Jack Ross and I am Acting Leader of the Labour Group on Wyverdale District Council, and although I hope to relinquish that post before long, I feel the need to set the record straight. In view of the Council and the Labour Group becoming willy-nilly one of the whipping boys in this Inquiry.

WATTS. Mr Ross, I'm delighted we can get your take on some of the suggestions that have been suggested in submissions during the course of this Inquiry.

JACK. Well, I'm sure you are.

WATTS. And while it's not true that the Council has become a whipping boy, there is a central claim I'd like you to address.

JACK. And what might that be?

WATTS. That by commission and omission, the Council contributed to the creation of a kind of cultural apartheid here in Wyverdale.

JACK. Oh, in what way?

WATTS. The first claim is that over many years the Council contributed to the segregation of its white and Asian communities by its housing policies.

JACK. You mean, why did we tend not to offer Asian families accommodation on the Morrison estate?

WATTS. Yes, if you like.

JACK. Well, I'd say that question contains its own answer, wouldn't you?

WATTS. More recently, it's been suggested that by targeting regeneration money at, particularly, Broughton Moor, the Council provoked resentment among residents of other districts, who felt their needs and problems were ignored.

JACK. What are you saying? There was cash available for Broughton Moor and we should have turned it down?

WATTS. There is also a contention that Council policies on grants to voluntary bodies, and its expenditure on translating Council literature, that the Council failed robustly to defend these / policies, and thus . . .

JACK. Look. We were told to do these things. Some of them were good. Some of them you could say were long overdue. But at the same time we were told to make cuts and farm out services and send hundreds of our people down the road. And the result of that was that last May, we lost power.

WATTS. And are you claiming that was / as a result of those –

JACK. But in fact of course, we'd already given it away. First to our 'advisor' from the Office of the Deputy Prime Minister. And then, on her instructions, to a new authority.

FRANK WILKINS *in the waiting area.*

And here he is. Can I go now?

Blackout.

Lights. FRANK WILKINS *in the witness area. The only councillor left is* DEREK. RIAZ *is still there. Two new members of the* PUBLIC *could be there, as is* LES.

STANLEY. Mr Wilkins, thank you for agreeing to speak to the Inquiry.

FRANK. It's my pleasure.

STANLEY. This is Mrs Watts, Counsel to the Inquiry.

FRANK. How do you do.

During the following, ALEX *enters. She is dressed as she was at the beginning of the play, colourfully and informally. She avoids* DEREK's *eye, but goes to* RIAZ, *puts her hand on his shoulder. He turns, looks round, pleased to see her, friendly but not intimate. She mimes phoning, he gives her the thumbs up, and she goes to the witness waiting area.*

WATTS. Mr Wilkins, I want to ask you first about your statement, at the Holocaust memorial ceremony in January, which is agreed to be one of the events that led up to the riot.

FRANK. Oh, is it?

WATTS. Is it what?

FRANK. Agreed.

WATTS. I think so.

FRANK. Well, you should ask the people who are of that opinion.

WATTS. Mr Wilkins, I'm asking you because your statement is thought to have been seriously divisive. For instance, the allegation that the Asian populations of the town were privileged by Council policies.

FRANK. The allegation?

WATTS. Yes.

FRANK. What makes you think it was an allegation?

WATTS. Well, in the sense that / people –

FRANK. I would say it was an exact summation of the facts.

WATTS. Well, Mr Wilkins, we can certainly go through / what you alleged –

FRANK. But if you can demonstrate that there were inaccuracies, I'm happy to discuss them.

STANLEY. Mr Wilkins, I understand that you're resistant / to this line of questioning –

FRANK. But without wishing to pull rank, or stand on ceremony, I'm sure you'll understand that I find it at the very least discourteous that you have chosen not to call me by my title.

WATTS. Sorry?

FRANK. Which is not a matter, obviously, of the fact I hold it. But of what the existence of that title and that office tells us about what happened here, over many months and years. Very shortly after these events occurred, I was elected Mayor of Wyverdale. Which is why I make this point to you.

He glances at ALEX, *who glares at him. Then he turns back.*

Suddenly, the Inquiry disappears and images of riot swirl across the stage, echoing the entry of the town in the third scene of the play. POLICEMEN *with shields, running* BYSTANDERS, YOUNG MEN *with scarves across their faces. Sirens, shouting and chanting, helicopter engines, drumming of truncheons on shields. Maybe, at the climax, a train of hijacked supermarket trolleys careers wildly across the stage.*

Scene Two

Six months earlier. Around 7.00pm on Sunday 23rd April, the lobby of the George Hotel. Upstage, the frontage door; downstage, easy chairs and tables. In both areas, various exits to other parts of the hotel: other locations include the reception, the annexe and the rooms upstairs, the Howard Suite and the ballroom, and the kitchens. During the scene, the noise of riot will increase outside.

As the lobby emerges from the swirl so too does ALEX, *looking miraculously different from a moment ago, now back in her Act One style and manner, standing near her suitcase, talking on her mobile phone.*

ALEX (*phone*). Hallo? Yeah, I'm keen not to miss yours either. I'm in the lobby at the George, it's 18.52 precisely, if you're at the civic, can I see you after it, and if you're not I'm in need of reassurance you're all right.

KURSHID HAFIZ has entered quickly from the frontage entrance. He has a jacket over a bloody shirt and an injured hand.

KURSHID. Excuse me.

ALEX (*closing her phone and turning to him*). Yes?

KURSHID. Uh, do you work here?

ALEX. No, but it sometimes seems that way.

Seeing KURSHID's *blood.*

Look, do you need some help? Can I call an ambulance?

KURSHID. It looks worse than it is.

ALEX. Well, at the very least . . .

Enter MICHAEL, *the waiter from the ballroom, with a tray of used, empty glasses.*

Ah, Michael. Do you have a first-aid kit?

MICHAEL. Uh – think so.

ALEX *takes the tray so that* MICHAEL *can go out to look for the first-aid kit in the reception area. She puts it down, as:*

ALEX. So what happened?

KURSHID. There's some guys what've been arrested, and there's a march down Northgate, and the coppers are trying to stop it.

ALEX (*looking towards the door*). How far down Northgate?

Sounds of sirens and shouting as MICHAEL *re-enters with a first-aid kit.*

KURSHID. That far.

MICHAEL *gives him the kit.*

MICHAEL. Here it is.

KURSHID. Ta.

ALEX (*gesturing to* KURSHID*'s injuries*). And, look . . . can you let him have twenty minutes in a room?

MICHAEL (*alarmed*). A room? I'm not sure, like . . .

ALEX. Come on.

After a deep breath, MICHAEL *goes out.*

(*To* KURSHID.) I mean, what happened, like, to you.

KURSHID *looks at her.*

KURSHID. Hey, don't I know you?

ALEX. Yes, you do. You thought I wanted to teach prostitutes karate.

MICHAEL *re-enters with a key.*

MICHAEL. Just twenty minutes, mind. And I'll have to swap the towels after. And don't touch the bed.

Handing over the selected key:

Room 307.

KURSHID. Thanks.

Enter MRS HATCHARD *the manageress, in a hurry.*

MRS HATCHARD. What's going on?

KURSHID *delicately hides his injuries and the key.*

MICHAEL. He's – uh, late for the affair.

MRS HATCHARD. Well, show the gentleman . . .

MICHAEL. Right.

MRS HATCHARD (*spotting the tray*). Michael.

MICHAEL *goes to the tray.* ALEX *nods to* KURSHID *who goes quickly out.*

MICHAEL. Sorry, Mrs Hatchard.

MICHAEL *picks up the tray and goes out.* MRS HATCHARD *turns back to* ALEX, *faintly surprised to see no* KURSHID.

MRS HATCHARD. Oh.

ALEX. Good evening.

MRS HATCHARD. Good evening.

Slight pause.

Now, am I right, you've stopped with us?

ALEX. Yes, many times.

Gesturing to her cases:

In fact . . .

MRS HATCHARD. Of course. You're the one with the chauffeur.

A POLICEMAN *and* POLICEWOMAN, *both constable rank, enter from the frontage as* KURSHID *goes out towards the rooms.*

POLICEMAN (*to* ALEX). Right then. Are you in charge here?

ALEX *gestures to* MRS HATCHARD.

Right madam. We've got a problem, like we've got a riot, beg its pardon – a disturbance, fifty yards up Northgate and I think we're going to have to have you shut up shop.

MRS HATCHARD. What, now?

The POLICEMAN*'s walkie-talkie squawks. He answers it.*

POLICEMAN. Excuse me.

POLICEWOMAN. How many guests?

MRS HATCHARD. Not many, it's a Sunday. But we've got two functions.

POLICEMAN (*walkie-talkie*). No, I'm at the George.

POLICEWOMAN. What functions?

POLICEMAN (*walkie-talkie*). Well, there's seven kinds of shit breaking loose outside.

MRS HATCHARD. One's a themed affair, that's the annexe, and the other one's a civic in the ballroom here.

POLICEWOMAN. So where's the annexe?

POLICEMAN (*walkie-talkie*). Well, that's bloody great, that is.

End walkie-talkie.

It looks like trouble out the back, in Brindley Passage.

POLICEWOMAN. There's two functions. One in the ballroom and the other in the annexe. Shall I do the annexe?

POLICEMAN. What's in the ballroom?

MRS HATCHARD. As I said, it's a civic. For St George. Mayor and councillors and a celebrity.

Enter RIAZ *from the frontage.*

POLICEMAN. OK, let's go.

Sees RIAZ*:*

And who are you?

RIAZ. I'm Councillor Rafique.

POLICEMAN. Well, we're advising everyone that for security reasons we cannot guarantee security. And so hence we're going to lock that door.

He nods to MRS HATCHARD, *who takes out her front door key and goes with the* POLICEMAN *to the frontage door, as* MICHAEL *enters from the kitchens with a full tray of various drinks.*

POLICEWOMAN (*to* MICHAEL). The annexe?

MICHAEL. Right.

MICHAEL puts down the tray and goes out with the POLICEWOMAN towards the annexe, leaving ALEX and RIAZ alone. ALEX's kisses RIAZ. Exhausted, RIAZ sits down.

ALEX. Where have you been?

RIAZ. Why are you here?

ALEX. I have a meeting.

RIAZ. So did I.

ALEX. Not – not the civic.

RIAZ. No.

ALEX. What's happening?

RIAZ. You haven't heard?

ALEX. Well, I know what's *happening*, obviously.

RIAZ. Yes.

The POLICEMAN and MRS HATCHARD come back from the frontage door, MRS HATCHARD then leading the POLICEMAN out towards the ballroom.

MRS HATCHARD. It's this way. I think they're in the middle of the speeches.

They're gone.

ALEX. And so?

RIAZ. And so what's happening is happening.

ALEX. And?

RIAZ. And I'm telephoned and I head off to the copshop to find out who's been arrested and when they'll be bailed. And it takes them the best part of an hour to tell me they were moved off to the centre the best part of an hour before.

ALEX. And so, what?

RIAZ. I tell the crowd outside the station.

ALEX. And?

RIAZ. Well, I'm hardly crowned with laurel leaves.

ALEX. But surely . . .

RIAZ. And then, guess what, someone in full Asian gets up and tells the crowd that I found the money for the prostitution centre and I'm in the pocket of the infidel.

ALEX. Well, I hope you / told them –

RIAZ. Oh, and that I said that using ASBOs is just another way of putting girls in jail.

ALEX. I said that.

RIAZ. Yes, you did.

Pause. He takes a glass of wine from MICHAEL*'s abandoned drinks tray and drinks it off.*

I can't see what you see in this.

ALEX. Well, you're not supposed to . . . And I doubt that it's a particularly choice example.

She goes to him, puts her hand on his shoulder.

Look, I'm sorry.

Pause. He softens a little.

Look, when this is over. Or resolved. Or both or neither. Can you not find another pressing reason for an overnight in the metropolis? If not a long weekend?

RIAZ. Alex, obviously I can't.

ALEX. Well, I didn't mean – like – now.

RIAZ. I did.

Pause.

ALEX. What do you mean?

RIAZ. I mean that I can't do this now.

ALEX. Now in the sense of . . .

RIAZ. . . . current circumstances.

ALEX. Because you're running. I mean, 'for office', obviously.

RIAZ. Alex, I'm not going to run for mayor.

ALEX. Why not? Because of this?

The riot, then the relationship:

Because of *this*?

RIAZ. Look, Alex, I . . .

ALEX. Oh, I'm sorry. Obviously. You need to be 'back home with your people'.

RIAZ. Please tell me, what is my alternative?

ALEX. I would have thought that's pretty obvious.

RIAZ. Oh, what? The 16.20 via Wakefield?

FRANK WILKINS enters unnoticed upstage.

ALEX. Why not? If you're not running, then why not? Particularly as my role in Wyverdale's affairs is now . . . by which of course, I mean . . .

She looks at RIAZ.

Riaz Rafique. Please tell me you're not running from this thing because I've got a child and I'm no longer with his father.

RIAZ. Alex, why are you here?

FRANK. Now, I think I can help with that.

ALEX (*turning to FRANK*). Ah.

FRANK (*glance at his watch*). I'm a little early, I'm afraid. The Leader was embarking on his introduction to the Mayor's welcome to our visiting celebrity. In view of what appears to be happening out there, I rather doubt they'll get to her.

Nodding to RIAZ:

Well. Councillor Rafique.

RIAZ. I'm sorry. I have to make my mind up what to do.

He takes a step towards the frontage door, remembers it's locked, and goes out the other way. ALEX looks after him, then turns back to FRANK, defiantly.

FRANK. So, 'a brief word in the George at seven'.

ALEX. The mayoral election.

FRANK. Yes?

ALEX. I think what you're doing is a terrible and dangerous idea.

FRANK. But it was yours. Imposed on us by the Secretary of State under the provisions of the Local Government Act 2000. And then endorsed by a comfortable margin of popular opinion. Unless you're saying that / it has to be –

ALEX. I naturally looked up Matthew chapter 21 verse 42.

FRANK. Aha.

ALEX. 'The stone that the builders rejected, the same is become the head of the corner.'

FRANK. *Which* they rejected.

ALEX. Quite.

Pause.

FRANK. You mean?

ALEX. I mean that all of this is simply vengeance.

FRANK. Actually, not quite.

ALEX. That you are proposing intervening in an electoral campaign, which even without *this*, (*The riot.*) will be obviously deeply, massively divisive, if not actually . . .

She stops herself, seeing the entrance of the civic reception which consists of GEORGE, JACK, ARTHUR, and the MAYOR; BARRY, YUSUF, MRS CHOWDURY, STEPHEN CROFT, TIM LAUNDIMER and the visiting celebrity, SUE BRAITHWAITE; MRS HATCHARD and the POLICEMAN; a young radio reporter called SHAZ; and other COUNCILLORS and DIGNITARIES and maybe STAFF.

SHAZ. A riot? There's a riot and no one tells me?

To FRANK:

Where's the riot?

FRANK gives an all-around gesture. By now GUESTS are turning on their phones, and taking and receiving messages and calls.

POLICEMAN. Right, gents and ladies, here's the situation. Nobody's in any present danger.

SHAZ (*to* ALEX). They made me switch my phone off.

ALEX. Right.

JACK. Well, hallo, Frank.

SHAZ. It's some kind of – council rule.

BARRY (*phone*). Hallo? This is Barry Ings. / Can I speak to the Duty Officer.

POLICEMAN. However, there's disorder out in Northgate, and so we're going to get you out, um . . .

SHAZ. Northgate.

She heads off towards the reception.

BARRY. Hallo, Tom? It's Barry Ings. / What gives?

MRS HATCHARD. Via the kitchens.

STEPHEN. Alex.

ALEX. Minister.

STEPHEN. So why are you . . .

STEPHEN's phone goes, so he takes it.

(*Phone.*) Hallo?

POLICEMAN. I just need to check the current state of things in / – where?

MRS HATCHARD. The kitchens exit into King Street.

FRANK. Now Martin Luther King Street.

POLICEMAN. Right.

He's about to go on walkie-talkie when the POLICEWOMAN *enters with* MICHAEL.

POLICEWOMAN. Ted, the anniversary's all out except the band.

POLICEMAN. Can you check the kitchen exit?

POLICEWOMAN. Fine.

BARRY (*phone*). Well, if that changes, call my mobile.

The POLICEWOMAN *goes out with* MRS HATCHARD *as the* POLICEMAN *speaks down his walkie-talkie:*

POLICEMAN. Hallo?

SHAZ *re-enters, and collars* TIM LAUNDIMER:

SHAZ. Where's Northgate?

TIM (*gestures to the locked frontage door*). There. But . . .

SHAZ *heads determinedly to the frontage door and, during the following, tries to open it.* GEORGE *comes to* ALEX. *He is clearly very upset about what's happening.*

GEORGE. Well, Alex, here you are.

ALEX. Yes.

GEORGE. And here's this.

GEORGE *walks away, as the* MAYOR *brings* SUE BRAITHWAITE *over to* ALEX, *followed by* BARRY INGS.

MAYOR. Now, Miss, um – you'll be wanting to meet our celebrity.

SUE (*hand out*). Sue Braithwaite.

ALEX (*shakes*). Alex Clifton.

MAYOR. She's starring in a current leading soap.

ALEX. Oh, yes?

BARRY. Despite her humble origins in Casterdyke.

SUE. Actually, at present, I'm serving life for matricide.

JACK *joining the group as* SHAZ *comes back down from the frontage door.*

SHAZ. Look, I'm sorry, but the Door is Locked.

POLICEMAN. Too right.

SHAZ. I demand you open up this door.

POLICEMAN. No, Miss.

The POLICEWOMAN *and* MRS HATCHARD *come back in from the kitchens.*

GEORGE. So this is . . . ?

JACK. Local radio . . . And, actually, George . . .

POLICEWOMAN (*to the* POLICEMAN). It's fine, if now.

JACK. You ought to make a statement.

GEORGE. Oh, do you think so?

POLICEMAN. Now everybody . . .

JACK. Obviously.

GEORGE. Right then.

POLICEMAN. Now everybody, we are going to get you, in an orderly and methodic manner, out of here.

MRS CHOWDURY. Good.

GEORGE (*to* SHAZ). I'm George Aldred. Do you want an interview?

SHAZ. Uh, George . . . ?

ARTHUR. The Leader of the Council.

SHAZ. Oh, right. Awesome.

STEPHEN CROFT *is consulting* MRS HATCHARD.

STEPHEN. Excuse me, I'm in, what? The private car park.

MRS HATCHARD. Then you'll need a token.

She's heading out to the reception desk.

GEORGE (*to* MRS HATCHARD). Peggy, is the Howard open?

MRS HATCHARD (*turning back*). Surely. Why?

POLICEMAN. I'll need to check out what you're driving into.

POLICEWOMAN (*urgency*). Ted . . .

GEORGE. I'm giving this young lady here an interview.

As GEORGE *and* SHAZ *go out towards the Howard Suite:*

SHAZ. See, it's my first major civil uprising.

GEORGE. Ours too.

POLICEMAN. Right. Everybody who's not in the car park . . . Please follow me.

SUE. Actually, my stuff is in my room . . .

MRS HATCHARD (*remembering she needs to get* STEPHEN's *token*). Token.

> MRS HATCHARD *goes out to the reception,* SUE BRAITHWAITE *goes out towards the rooms.*

ARTHUR (*to* JACK). You coming, Jack?

JACK. No, I'll wait for George.

POLICEWOMAN. Don't try to leave while we get back.

> *The* POLICEMAN *and* POLICEWOMAN *leave with everyone except* STEPHEN, ALEX, JACK, FRANK, ARTHUR *and* MICHAEL. ALEX *stops* YUSUF:

ALEX. Um, Mr Iqbal?

YUSUF. Yes?

ALEX. It was me who said that using ASBOs against prostitutes was just another way of putting them in jail.

YUSUF. Come again?

ALEX. It was me. Not Councillor Rafique.

> YUSUF *looks at* ALEX, *blankly. Then he turns and goes. After a moment:*

ARTHUR. Well, here we are. Once again, our town performing its historic role. Of making everybody else look good.

> *He is heading to go out.* MRS HATCHARD *comes back in, handing* STEPHEN *his token.*

MRS HATCHARD. I'm afraid I've had to close the bar, on the grounds of health and safety.

> *She gestures at* MICHAEL's *tray of drinks.*

But you're very welcome.

ARTHUR. Well, in that case, sod it.

> *He goes and gets a drink.*

MRS HATCHARD. I'm in reception. Presuming that at some point this will end.

> MRS HATCHARD *goes out, having a discreet word with* MICHAEL, *who comes forward to hand round drinks.*

ARTHUR. No, it's all right, lad. We can help oursen.

There's a banging on the door. MICHAEL *moves to the side, to keep an eye on things.*

ALEX. What's that?

MICHAEL. I, uh . . .

JACK. I'll take a look.

JACK goes to the frontage door.

FRANK. Or: they promise us we can be Islington and we turn into Beirut.

STEPHEN (*to* ALEX). So why are you . . .

ALEX (*to* STEPHEN). I'll tell you later.

JACK's back.

JACK. It's Anwar Hafiz and Derek Morley.

To MICHAEL:

The keys.

MICHAEL. Uh, actually . . .

JACK. The keys or let them in.

MICHAEL *goes out to get the keys as* FRANK *moves in on* STEPHEN.

FRANK. Well, Minister, I gather that congratulations are in order.

STEPHEN. It's a sideways move.

FRANK. But eminently appropriate, as it's turned out.

STEPHEN. Yes.

MICHAEL *comes back in with the keys, then goes with* JACK *to let in* ANWAR *and* DEREK.

FRANK. Don't they say about the Home Office, it's like Millwall Football Club?

STEPHEN. I have heard that.

FRANK. 'Nobody likes us, we don't care.'

With MICHAEL *and* JACK, ANWAR *and* DEREK *come down from the door.*

ALEX. Are you all right?

STEPHEN. What's happening?

ALEX (*to* ANWAR, *gesturing to drinks*). Do you want a drink?

ANWAR goes to the drinks tray, takes an orange juice and drinks it in one.

JACK (*to* DEREK). Well?

DEREK (*taking a beer, to* ANWAR). You tell 'em.

ANWAR. Well . . .

Suddenly, the frontage door bursts open and a young ASIAN MAN bursts in, a scarf over his face. He looks at the assembly.

ARTHUR. Yes, lad?

The ASIAN MAN *runs back out.* MICHAEL *goes quickly and locks the door.*

ANWAR. Well, at first, there is fighting outside the Nelson pub and several arrests are made. A crowd gathers at the police station and demands that the arrested young men be released.

DEREK. But actually, / they was moved –

ANWAR. But in fact the prisoners are never there, they'd been taken to the centre. So then the angry crowd attacks the hang-out centre for the prostitutes.

FRANK. Well, well.

ALEX. And?

DEREK. And the main group's now twenty yards up Northgate, fighting with a line of police with shields. It's a miracle we got in here at all.

JACK. Who's winning?

ANWAR. Well, there are no signs of the rioters dispersing. Also I understand there are young men defending Broughton Moor from attacks from the Crazy Gang or other white lads from the Morrison estate.

STEPHEN. The Crazy Gang?

JACK. Football hooligans.

STEPHEN. I see. So how did it begin?

ANWAR's phone goes.

ANWAR. Excuse me.

He takes the call:

Hallo?

GEORGE *and* SHAZ *re-enter from the Howard Suite. She's packed up her equipment in her shoulder bag and is talking on her mobile phone.*

SHAZ *(phone).* It's Shaz. Yeah, I got the Leader.

ANWAR *(phone, Urdu).* Kurshid, tu hotel me ho? Kidhar? [Kurshid, you're in the hotel? Where?]

SHAZ *(phone).* Ay, I'll be straight back.

She ends the call.

GEORGE. What's happening?

SHAZ. So where's the exit?

ANWAR *(phone).* 307.

ALEX. Through the kitchen.

SHAZ. Cool.

ANWAR *(phone, Urdu).* Udhar raho. [Wait there.]

MICHAEL. But the coppers say that you've to wait.

SHAZ. Well, bugger that.

ANWAR. Forgive me please.

He slips quickly out towards the rooms.

SHAZ *(waving her phone).* They've torched a post office and a car place.

ANWAR. The Mercedes showroom?

SHAZ. Didn't say.

To GEORGE:

And hey, thanks for the, like, exclusive.

She hurries out, MICHAEL *following.*

JACK *(to* GEORGE). What 'like exclusive'?

GEORGE *takes a half of lager and drinks it.*

STEPHEN. So what did you say?

GEORGE. What you'd expect.

STEPHEN. What's that?

GEORGE. You know.

STEPHEN. We don't know, George.

GEORGE. A call for calm. Full backing for our lads in blue. Minority of hotheads, few bad apples, mustn't judge our youth by. The tradition of diversity and tolerance for which Wyverdale is famed.

Pause.

JACK. And then?

GEORGE. I thought of what I should've said.

JACK. And what was that?

GEORGE. Well, I guess that's it for the recovery. Ms Clifton's radiant future. That's all shot to buggery.

JACK. But you didn't say that.

GEORGE. No.

Pause.

STEPHEN. What did you say?

GEORGE. I quoted Arthur.

ARTHUR. Oh, ay?

GEORGE. I said I'd been a councillor in Wyverdale back while it weren't Wyverdale, and I can't think of a greater disavowal of what we've done as a council and I've done as a leader as what's going off out there.

ALEX. And?

GEORGE. And that when the district party meets tomorrow evening to select its candidate for Mayor, I'll not be putting up my name.

FRANK *laughs.*

ALEX. George, you can't do that.

GEORGE. Oh, no? Thought you'd be pleased. Give a free run to Councillor Rafique.

ARTHUR. The True Believer.

ALEX. George, things have changed.

Pause.

DEREK. What's up?

FRANK. I think Ms Clifton thinks there's something you should know.

JACK. What's that?

ALEX. He's running.

STEPHEN. What?

ALEX. For Mayor. Frank's running to be Mayor of Wyverdale.

FRANK. On behalf of course of its ordinary working folk.

JACK. But – *what*?

FRANK. Oh, did you all think I'd hop off to the opposition benches, sulk a bit and hop on back? Oh, Jack.

JACK. Well, I always said, you're your own worst enemy.

GEORGE. Not while I'm around.

FRANK. Which is why Ms Clifton came here, to persuade me not to stand. On the grounds, presumably, that my standing might turn this campaign into a real contest. As opposed to a mere coronation of . . . well, the proverbial in the red rosette. But now I fear I am intruding on a private grief. I believe the hotel has something they now call a mezzanine?

He goes out. Pause.

STEPHEN. So this selection meeting is tomorrow evening?

GEORGE. Ay.

JACK. Well, shall I say it? George, if we're up against Frank Wilkins, then you have to stand.

GEORGE. I disagree.

DEREK. Well, if he won't, we have to see we get the only other candidate who can.

ARTHUR. Oh, and who's that?

DEREK *gestures to* JACK.

Oh, is it, now?

GEORGE. Well, that makes sense to me.

ARTHUR. Well, it don't to me.

DEREK. Why not, Arthur?

ARTHUR. 'Cos if Frank Wilkins claims to speak for the ordinary working folk of Wyverdale, happen it's best we put one up oursen.

JACK. Arthur, you're not proposing you / stand for –

ARTHUR. And as we don't think the system's broke, and as we've a perfectly good Mayor in place already, I suggest that's who we go for.

JACK. Maureen Teale?

ARTHUR. That's right.

JACK. For the elected Mayor?

ARTHUR. Ay.

DEREK. Arthur, this is like executive. It's not just like opening supermarkets. The elected Mayor is like the Leader.

ARTHUR. Oh, and Wyverdale in't ready for a lady leader?

GEORGE. I've agreed a candidate's debate on Radio North.

ARTHUR. What's wrong with that?

JACK. Arthur, Maureen Teale can't string together a coherent English sentence.

DEREK. She can't read one out.

ARTHUR. Well, whatever. I'll not be party to a stitch-up. And Mo gets my vote.

Pause.

DEREK. Well, if it's an open field . . .

JACK. Yes, Derek?

DEREK. . . . then I think we should take a stand for multiracial Wyverdale.

Slight pause.

GEORGE. What, Riaz Rafique?

ARTHUR. You've changed your tune.

DEREK. No. Anwar Hafiz.

GEORGE. Or you could all stand. And it'd be Jack and his bloody chairs.

ARTHUR. I beg your pardon?

GEORGE. What were it? One lot supposed to put 'em in a circle, another lot turns 'em upside down and the third lot takes 'em to another room. Just like the Labour Group.

STEPHEN (*to* ALEX). What's this?

ALEX. Teamwork / exercise.

GEORGE. In fact, we could do it. Pass the time.

He knocks over a chair and gestures to the Howard Suite:

Bloody stacks of 'em in there.

JACK. Or maybe we should ask you if you'll change your mind.

A helicopter flies low over the hotel. They all look towards it.

GEORGE. I said why I won't stand. 'Cos I think we in here need to take responsibility for what's happening out there.

ARTHUR. Agreed. But I don't think it's 'we'.

They all look at ARTHUR.

Did I hear the Morrison estate's attacking Broughton Moor?

DEREK. Ay, Anwar said.

ARTHUR. Well, I wonder who's to blame for that.

Pause.

STEPHEN. What do you mean, Arthur?

ARTHUR. Who told us as we had to get up a translation unit. And spread largesse to, what? What did Frank say? The Kashmiri this, Islamic that.

STEPHEN. That was your decision.

ALEX. It was also right.

ARTHUR. And who got the Asian lads setting up vigilante patrols?

JACK. And provided them a target.

ALEX. If you mean the / drop-in centre –

ARTHUR. But if you really want to bugger things up, if you really want to light the blue touchpaper and retire, then have poor white and even poorer Asian areas competing to be more miserable and deprived than t'other.

ALEX. What are you saying? There was cash available and you shouldn't have accepted it?

ARTHUR. I'm saying as the Council takes the rap for everything and no doubt we'll take the rap for this and all. But I think we all know who's to blame.

ALEX. They were your decisions.

JACK. Ay, on pain of, what? 'The Czechoslovak Option'?

DEREK. And there's the elected Mayor.

ARTHUR. Which sure as hell weren't our / decision.

JACK. And do we think that 350-plus redundancies help promote an atmosphere of tolerance and mutual respect? Now she's had our housing benefit transferred to Nottingham?

ALEX. Now, look . . . Look, I . . .

STEPHEN. I'm sorry, what exactly are you saying here?

Pause. Enter SUE BRAITHWAITE, *changed and with her cases.* STEPHEN, *gesturing towards the riot:*

I mean, are you saying that outsourcing housing benefit is to blame for this?

JACK. If the cap . . .

STEPHEN. Are you saying, Alex . . . Are you saying, we're to blame for this?

GEORGE. No, no one's saying that.

ARTHUR. Speak for yourself.

STEPHEN. Because . . .

A big explosion from outside.

SUE. Uh – excuse me. But can someone get us out of here?

STEPHEN. Well, certainly, I've got a car . . .

A crash, and broken glass falls. Enter ANWAR *and*
KURSHID. *He has cleaned himself up, covered his shirt*
with his jacket, and has his injured hand in a pocket.

ARTHUR. Ay, up.

DEREK. Bloody hell.

STEPHEN. And I think, yes, that it might be time to go.

JACK, ARTHUR, DEREK *and* GEORGE *go to look at*
what's happening. ALEX *has gone to* KURSHID.

ALEX (*to* KURSHID). How are you? Are you all right?

ANWAR. He's fine. By coincidence my nephew Kurshid is
here in this very same hotel.

DEREK. Goes on like this, someone's going to get killed.

KURSHID. I'm – like – seeing friends.

ANWAR. Yes, he has friends involved in an anniversary affair.

JACK. They've moved on. It's a kind of running battle. They're
attacking TK Maxx . . .

DEREK. And Kwik Save.

KURSHID (*to* ALEX). I been here all evening.

ANWAR. You know, it is sometimes hard to know quite how
things start.

STEPHEN. Look, I do really think . . .

ANWAR. Maybe it is a councillor who is deceived and makes
a speech and a hothead takes his microphone. Or maybe it
is a banned march or new roofs or a hang-out place for
prostitutes. Or a translation unit or the need for a translation
unit. Or perhaps it is a man who comes out of a pub in his
local-team regalia. And perhaps he calls out 'Paki, make my
day.' And 'We know you, Paki, and why not fuck off back
to where you didn't come from?' And perhaps the Paki
takes him on. With predictable and immediate results. That
would be a night's work, would it not?

ALEX. You mean, one man comes out of the Admiral Nelson.

ANWAR. Wearing a football T-shirt.

ALEX. And he starts it off.

ARTHUR. Well, whatever.

ANWAR *says nothing.*

STEPHEN. So what's all this?

ALEX. And of course, you're going to tell the police.

ANWAR. No, I am not.

ALEX. Because, you see, I think . . .

ANWAR. Because of who the Paki was.

ALEX. But surely if / that's true –

ANWAR HAFIZ *sees the* POLICEMAN, SUPERINTENDENT RICKS *and* MICHAEL *enter.* KURSHID *delicately places his room key on the table.*

ANWAR. Thank goodness, it could not have been my nephew Kurshid. Who is here all evening in the anniversary affair.

RICKS. Councillor Aldred? I heard you were still here.

GEORGE. I were talking on the wireless.

RICKS. Now I need to get you out.

JACK. So what's the latest?

RICKS. There's not much left of the Merc concession. And it's spread to Thawston.

DEREK. Who's attacking what in Thawston?

RICKS. Who is the residents. What's, Royal Cabs, a corner shop, the Bangladeshi restaurant, and us.

ALEX. *The* Bangladeshi restaurant?

GEORGE. There's just the one. In fact, I think we gave 'em seven grand to start it up.

RICKS. So at present, it is Asians going for white stores in Broughton Moor and whites selecting Asian targets in Thawston. And my men in the middle. So, shall we go?

STEPHEN. I'm in the car park.

RICKS. Give us five minutes, I'll have someone at the barrier.

ALEX. In fact, I'm staying.

RICKS. Sorry?

ALEX. I have some – business to conduct.

RICKS. I can't advise that.

ALEX. Even so.

STEPHEN. Uh, George, a lift?

GEORGE. That'd be champion.

SUE. Um, I need getting to the station.

RICKS. Certainly.

JACK. Good evening, Comrades.

ANWAR (*to* ALEX *and* GEORGE). Time was, you had a civil uprising, you couldn't move for Women Against This or That. Defence Groups. 'Would you care to use our Roneo?'

ALEX. Well, I doubt, on this / occasion –

ARTHUR (*with one last withering gesture towards the riot outside*). Time was, we made the semifinals of the Cup.

RICKS *and the* POLICEMAN *lead out* ARTHUR, JACK, DEREK, ANWAR, KURSHID *and* SUE BRAITHWAITE. MICHAEL *sees* KURSHID*'s key on the table, picks it up, and goes out of the room, leaving* GEORGE, STEPHEN *and* ALEX *alone.*

STEPHEN. So what was that stuff about the Crazy Gang?

ALEX. It's the single-trigger theory. It's one man who comes out of one pub and shouts something at one Pakistani, who fights back. And wouldn't it be great if that was why this happened? Wouldn't that be awesome? But of course it isn't. Is it?

STEPHEN. Alex, you're not responsible for this.

ALEX. Oh, no?

STEPHEN. In what way are you responsible for this?

ALEX. 'I should be Chief Executive of a major London borough. I should remember why I'm not.'

GEORGE. I asked you about that.

ALEX (*to* STEPHEN). Well, maybe you should tell him.

Slight pause.

STEPHEN. When she went in, Alex found an ally in the newly elected Leader of the Council. He was by origin, I think, a Sikh. There was a group who didn't like him much, on any of those grounds, and they encouraged a white secretary to accuse him of harassment. And the Head of Personnel sat the girl down and persuaded her to withdraw the charge.

GEORGE. I don't quite get the problem.

STEPHEN. The charge was true. Well, true enough. And Alex told the Leader it was him or her. And the party sent a troubleshooter in from Walworth Road, ostensibly to bang the party's heads together, but actually to sit Alex down and say he understood what she was saying, but even so, if she wanted work in a Labour-controlled authority again, it might be better if she left a decent interval and then took a job with Civitatis.

ALEX. I didn't get the politics. You said it, George.

STEPHEN. And why did I do that? Because I thought that fighting racism trumped fighting sexism. That the standards we apply to middle-class white men don't apply to people who have suffered centuries of imperial exploitation. And I was wrong. And I think that we may reap the tares of what we sowed then, here today.

Pause.

GEORGE. And of course we told 'em Broughton Moor and Thawston were 'communities' with their own 'identities' which surely trumped being part of our society.

STEPHEN. Yes.

GEORGE. But it in't just whites in Thawston, who see Broughton get the bathrooms and the hanging baskets and they're getting nowt. It's, we have to match the funds and we have to carry on the youth work and the rehabilitation and the roofs when all your cash runs out, and where's that come from? Well, I tell you. It comes from things that everybody uses, swimming baths and libraries and yes, bloody refuse. And so the folk what votes for us – who 'choose us' in 'the democratic market-place' – these people can and do legitimately ask: if all we're doing's holding out the bowl for someone else's ladle, if we're not actually responsible for owt, then who gives a toss who runs the borough anyroad?

Slight pause.

And perhaps we should have said that, way back. But, up against the various alternatives on offer – from Leena Harvey Wells to the Czechoslovak Option – we decided all in all it were best to do what you wanted us to do.

STEPHEN. Eventually.

GEORGE. But then you said that weren't enough, we'd to believe in it and all. And so we did that too.

ALEX. Eventually.

GEORGE. But even that weren't good enough, you need your True Believer and you saddles us with the elected Mayor. And of course, you were dead right.

ALEX. Oh, yes?

GEORGE. Oh, ay. Because what you meant by thinking it were right, were thinking nothing else were right. Or could be right, or possible. Now then or ever. But some of us remembered when there was summat called a municipality, which built drains and cleared up filth and tended public parks, and it were run by folks called citizens on behalf of other citizens what voted for 'em. And they belonged to things called parties which held out summat called a vision, nay a goal, not summat could get sorted out today, nor even Tuesday week, nor maybe ever. But it held out the prospect and the means of things being different. For everyone, but most of all for people who can't play the cornet and whose lad in't getting snapped up by the Royal Ballet and who can't afford the 16.20 via Wakefield anyroad. But who, for all that, are still citizens and want to feel that what they do brings that vision a bit closer. And, sure, it turned out it weren't up to much, so we turned to customer delivery. And there's gains in that, for customers, but summat lost and all, and I don't think you got that. Don't think we got it. Got it now.

Enter FRANK.

ALEX. So what . . . what do you want? Which can be done today?

GEORGE, *aware of* FRANK, *gestures towards him without looking at him.*

GEORGE. I want you to stop Frank. 'Cos he *is* your fault. Or if you can't, you've to stop him shopping Jack. However much that might stick in your craw. 'Cos otherwise he'll bloody win. And all this – 'll be just for starters.

FRANK. Speaking of blame, how are we doing with what seems to be an attempt to ethnically cleanse the Pakistani parts of Broughton Moor? Unless you're saying that Society's responsible?

STEPHEN (*angered*). No, no one's saying that society's responsible for this.

GEORGE *makes to go. An afterthought:*

GEORGE. Eh, you know, t'in't Poland. T'in't Czechoslovakia. It's Kosovo.

ALEX. It's what?

GEORGE. You do the right thing, from the best of motives. But you do it from a height of fifteen thousand feet. Which means you hit a lot of things you didn't mean to, and you store us up all kinds of trouble for the future. And why do you do that? Simple. If you're that far up, we can't fire back at you.

Slight pause.

So tomorrow night, I'm going to vote for Anwar Hafiz. As he says, there were a time.

He goes and touches ALEX's *arm.*

When people like you put themselves in range.

GEORGE *goes out.* STEPHEN *follows.* ALEX *turns to* FRANK.

ALEX. 'To ethnically cleanse'?

FRANK. Why, don't you think / that's what's occurring?

ALEX. It's a split infinitive.

FRANK. While, strictly speaking, 'a few bad apples' doesn't
mean 'it's not a problem'. It means, that a small number of
bad fruit can corrupt the barrel.

ALEX. Yes. And you don't think that you standing for election,
now, would do just that?

FRANK. No more than Jack, I would have thought.

ALEX. Jack's not the issue.

FRANK. And I wonder, how much of what I want to say you
really disagree with? Honestly?

ALEX. Try me.

FRANK. That we made a dreadful error, telling people that
their identity overrode their membership of our society.
There being, as we all agree, such a thing as society. So
how are we doing so far?

ALEX. Well, that all depends on who you think 'we' are.

FRANK. All right. I'm running Broughton Girls, and I posit
the idea that all in all it might be mildly preferable for
young women to take some form of exercise, be it team
sports, swimming or whatever. And I receive a deputation –
all-male, obviously – which threatens to shop me to the
Council for cultural insensitivity. On the grounds, no doubt,
of centuries of white oppression. So what does the former
Press Officer of Stepney Women Against Racism think to
that?

ALEX. No, but as you know full well / those people –

FRANK. And I imagine on your travels round the borough you
stopped off in Fenleydale. With its little closes all called
things like Ivy Crescent, with their carriage lamps and
sloping eaves. And its pubs with faintly rural titles, like the
Hare and Hounds, but inside they're still spit and sawdust
and you realise they should be called the White Flight
Arms. And they're there because the other lot are here, and
they're mortgaged to the hilt, and they know the hilt they're
mortgaged to will disappear like morning mist the instant
there's an Ahmed or an Aziz in the street. And they don't
see why that has to happen. And I am saying, simply, that it
is important somebody, apart from Britannia, speaks for

them. And so, yes, I will pay attention to Jack Ross's grimy past. And no, I won't stand down.

ALEX. From this to that. From here to there. From yes, it would be good for people to learn English via sure, girls need to learn to swim and not be forced to marry people they don't want to, all the way to Let's Keep Ivy Crescent White.

FRANK. Well, as I say . . .

ALEX. And you really think you're the alternative to people like Britannia? As opposed to, simply, opening the door?

ALEX's phone goes. She answers it. As she speaks, FRANK goes and looks out towards the riot outside.

(*Phone.*) Hallo.

Yes. Yes, I heard.

You've made your mind up, fine.

But even so.

There's a pause before she closes the phone and ends the call.

FRANK. So let me guess. The problem's not your child, it's his. And the fact that his child's being brought up by his mother.

ALEX *looks away.*

And did he tell you why he won't run for the nomination?

ALEX. Well, I think that it's a variety of factors.

FRANK. Including 'Councillor Rafique, great friend to prostitutes and pimps.'

ALEX. Which is of course / ridiculous –

FRANK. And then, there's his ethnicity.

ALEX. What?

FRANK. Don't you know the football joke? 'Who do you support?' 'Everton and anyone but Liverpool.' In fact, it matters if you're from the next-door village. Riaz Rafique is a Bangladeshi in a Pakistani ward. Frankly, after this, I doubt that he'll get reselected.

ALEX (*making to go*). Quite.

FRANK. Just one more thing. I think it's proper your involvement in this election ends tonight.

ALEX turns back.

ALEX. Why should it?

FRANK. Well, you are a civil servant.

ALEX. Well, I think that's my decision.

FRANK. It was your decision to enter into an affair with the man who you promoted to my job.

Pause. ALEX takes this in.

ALEX. But I . . . I don't believe you.

FRANK. Try me.

Suddenly, from upstage, the BAND from the themed anniversary enters, carrying their equipment. The theme is Country and Western and the band consists of BRAD, a white man in his 20s, CHLOË from the nail shop and a then clean-shaven FAZAL MANSOOR, who's trying to make a phone call. Till she speaks, ALEX stands, a little distant, trying to work out what to do.

BRAD. Hey, there are some people.

FRANK. Yes, there are some people.

CHLOË. I still say we should've left the stuff and come back later.

FAZAL (*phone*). Hallo?

BRAD. Fuck, did anyone pick up the amp leads?

CHLOË. Faz?

FAZAL. I'm on the phone.

CHLOË. I can see you're on the phone. We're also trapped in the hotel from hell surrounded by a fucking riot.

FAZAL. Anyway, I need to make this call.

BRAD. I'll get 'em.

He goes out.

FAZAL. Oh, for fuck's sake.

FRANK. So you're the themed affair.

CHLOË. Well, we were playing at it. We're the Tex Mex Boogie Band.

FRANK. I'm pleased to meet you.

FAZAL. I still can't get fucking through. What's the point of being able to beam videos to Jupiter if you can't call Thawston High Street?

CHLOË. We're really fusion. But tonight we've kind of been effectively a Jim Reeves Tribute Band.

FRANK. I'm pleased.

CHLOË. I'm not. It's fucking crap.

FAZAL. This is a fucking pisstake anyway.

Re-enter BRAD *with the leads.*

BRAD. OK. You want summat doing, go and do it.

FAZAL (*to* BRAD). Plonker.

ALEX (*to* FAZAL). What's happening?

FAZAL. It's my folks. It don't matter anyway. It's just they're always there. I mean, for fuck's sake, they run a fucking restaurant.

BRAD. Now shall we go?

ALEX. In Thawston.

FAZAL. Yuh.

ALEX. Your parents run a restaurant, in Thawston.

FAZAL. S'right. There's just the one. So what?

Slight pause.

BRAD. So how the fuck do we get out of here?

FRANK. You go out through the kitchens. That way.

ALEX (*to* FAZAL). What's your name?

FAZAL (*why ask?*). My name? It's Faz.

CHLOË (*enjoying the sound*). 'Fazal Mansoor. In the name of God, the most compassionate, / the merciful . . . '

FAZAL. So there's a problem?

ALEX. Faz. You should . . . you must . . .

To the OTHERS:

Please, take him home.

Slight pause.

BRAD. And are we going to get there? Now or fucking ever?

FAZAL. Right.

CHLOË, BRAD *and* FAZAL *go out, carrying their equipment.* ALEX *turns to* FRANK.

FRANK. You didn't tell him.

ALEX. Nor did you.

FRANK (*riot*). I don't think this is my responsibility.

ALEX. No, but you think it's mine. Which is why I have to make my mind up what to do.

Unexpectedly, she goes out, towards the Howard Suite.

FRANK. Ms Clifton?

Even more unexpectedly, ALEX *pulls in a stack of chairs, from the Howard Suite.*

ALEX. 'Cos I don't think we're to blame but I do think we're responsible. And, of course, the cause that matters is the cause you can address.

She takes one of the chairs, turns it upside down, takes it downstage and puts it on the floor.

And I'm told, if you want to foster tolerance and understanding, the thing you've absolutely got to do is to provide a site that's new for everyone.

She goes and takes another chair, upends it, and lays it by the first.

I mean, apparently, there's no point force-feeding one lot chicken dansak while you're frogmarching the others off to cheer the lads at Broughton Park.

We realise that she is forming the chairs into a circle, upside down, across the room.

FRANK. Uh, Ms Clifton, what exactly . . .

ALEX. And Tai Chi's fine, but it's really for old people, and
there's karate, but I haven't kept it up . . . Though I was in
Malaysia and there was this wedding and the entertainment
was a dancey thing called – Silat? – which seemed to be a
kind of martial art done really slowly . . . And for fuck's
sake, if Taekwondo's an Olympic discipline there has to be
a Silat instructor somewhere.

The circle of chairs is nearly complete.

'Cos is a civil servant teaching white kids Asian dance more
improbable that a Bangladeshi Muslim in a temporary Jim
Reeves tribute band. Or a small boy hiding underneath his
father's bed with a tube of English mustard, being guarded
by an Asian youth whatever or the Anti-Racist this or that.
And as you point out, time was, I was there.

Slight pause.

And it's actually pretty simple. You go into a different
room. And you turn yourself the other way up. And you
stand inside the circle, and you put yourself in range.

Slight pause.

And thereby you give yourself the right to say there must
be – there must always be – an alternative to going back
home to your people.

She stands, holding the last chair, looking at FRANK. *She
looks a little like she did when she held the wreath at the
end of Act One.*

And you're right. I can hear me in you. And I can't have
that. So if you stand, I'll stay. In fact, I'll stay as long as
you do. Way beyond a week next Tuesday. Yes. That's what
I have to do.

She puts the last chair down.

Blackout.

End of play.

Afterword

Race and Multiculturalism in British Politics

One of the unexpected consequences of the fall of the Berlin Wall was a renewal of the fortunes of Europe's far right. Initially, the collapse of communism appeared to promise a new, expanded, supernational Europe, in which the old walls, barriers and borders which had caused so much bloodshed in the past would melt in the summer sunshine. In fact, this dream was quickly undermined, first by a rise of nationalism among the newly liberated populations of the east, where previously incorporated republics like Estonia, Latvia, Slovenia and the Ukraine declared their independence and set about reviving old national anthems and street names, designing new currency and postage stamps, and appointing commissions to ensure that their languages were made as distinct as possible from those of their neighbours. Then this new nationalism began to influence parts of western Europe that wanted to be free of national oppression (like Wales and Scotland), or from the burden of supporting less-developed parts of their national state (as in Lombardy and Bavaria) or both (as in Catalonia).

The second development was the renewal of the far right – as an electoral force in France, Belgium, Italy, Holland, Denmark and Austria, and as a violent force in Sweden and the former East Germany, where attacks on refugees reached murderous levels in the early '90s. Differing widely on issues ranging from EU membership to homosexuality, what all these movements had and have in common is a hostility to foreigners, a hostility made more acute by the expansion of the Union in 2004. The results of the 2004 Euro-elections – in which the far-right bloc at Strasbourg increased from 24 to 57 – demonstrated that immigration remains a potent issue across the continent.

Alone among the major European countries, Britain has never had a far-right MEP. Throughout the '90s, while 'post-fascism' was on the march on the continent (joining the government in Italy, supporting it in Denmark), the British National Party and its various rivals and offshoots remained electorally insignificant. To explain this, people pointed to a number of factors. The first was our first-past-the-post electoral system, traditionally hostile to small parties. The second was that a neo-fascist upsurge in the 1970s – spearheaded by the National Front – was exposed and defeated by a strong anti-fascist movement between 1976 and 1979, driving it underground in disarray. A third was that in the same period a renewed Conservative Party under Margaret Thatcher articulated the same concerns in more moderate language – both promising to halt a tide of people threatening to swamp Britain with an 'alien culture' and pledging to reverse national decline. But the most significant factor was the nature of British immigration.

The clearest comparison is with France and Germany. In France, immigrants are traditionally granted full citizenship rights, but expected fully to embrace French culture. In Germany, the guest-worker was allowed to do anything he or she liked culturally, but not to become a full citizen. In Britain, immigrants from the former imperial possessions in the Caribbean and the Asian sub-continent were at first asked to assimilate (on the French model). But by the mid-'60s a compromise had emerged, best summed up in Home Secretary Roy Jenkins' 1966 definition of integration 'not as a flattening process of assimilation but as equal opportunity, accompanied by cultural diversity, in an atmosphere of mutual tolerance'. Granted the vote but not required to abandon their dress, religion or cuisine, Caribbean and Asian immigrants were constitutionally enabled (if not always encouraged) to enter mainstream British life. Partly as a result of those tools, but mainly as a result of their own political and industrial efforts, immigrants overcame prejudice and resistance in business, the professions, culture, sport, but most of all in the trade unions and the Labour Party, in order to achieve a place in mainstream British life that was denied to culturally-isolated North Africans in France or disenfranchised Turkish guest-workers in Germany. One of the many happy results of this was that the British far right could never gain a toe-hold. Indeed the British National Party's defining policy – the compulsory repatriation of all non-white immigrants, their dependents and descendents

– eventually became so ridiculous that they were forced to abandon it.

That rosy view of a smooth progression from monocultural '50s Britain to a multiracial paradise today is of course an exaggeration. The creation of a reasonably workable multi-cultural society in Britain is a real if incomplete achievement. But, back to the '60s, the journey has been punctuated by dramatic setbacks and abrupt changes of direction.

Roy Jenkins' liberal attitude and policies were first challenged by maverick conservative MP Enoch Powell, whose 'Rivers of Blood' speech in April 1968 attacked mass immigration and the race-relations legislation that sought to cement Jenkins' vision. The result of Powell's speech – and the two general elections which they influenced – added a major rider to Jenkins' strategy. Both major parties agreed that in order for integration to work, mass immigration had to stop. In the '70s, declining primary immigration 'allowed' equality measures to be introduced at home (notably in a beefed-up Race Relations Act in 1976); more profoundly, Jenkins' commitment to cultural diversity led to a theory of cultural pluralism which was satirised as the 'three Ss' – saris, samosas and steel bands – but which held as a principle that Britain had moved from a monocultural to a multicultural society, in which many cultures of equal value could and should coexist. The derisory National Front vote in the 1979 General Election appeared to confirm that the three Ss were working.

This confidence was undermined in 1981 when Britain's then worst race riots broke out in largely Afro-Caribbean Brixton and Liverpool and largely South-Asian Southall. The Scarman Report into the riots is now regarded as mild if not measly by anti-racist campaigners, but at the time it established two important principles: that the attitude and practice of a section of the police (albeit as individuals rather than an institution) was racially prejudiced, and that black and Asian communities suffered from racial disadvantage, which prevented Jenkins-style integration to occur. In this context, saris and samosas looked like a fig-leaf and the focus of public policy – particularly in local government, where Labour was in power – shifted to anti-racism. Left-wing councils in London and elsewhere defined racism as 'prejudice-plus-power' – hostile attitudes by people in a position to make people's lives worse –

and set out to challenge racist attitudes among their employees. At the same time, they applied culturally pluralist principles to their dealings with black and Asian communities, encouraging them to develop their self-identity by providing grants to their organisations.

These twin policies quickly came under attack from right and left. From the right, the tabloid press sought to 'expose' the activities of what it called 'loony left Labour councils' in eliminating pejorative racial language – the classic example was the pillorying of a local authority which supposedly banned children singing the nursery rhyme 'Baa Baa Black Sheep'. There were a number of incidents – notably in the North London borough of Brent – in which 'heroic' individual teachers could be painted as martyrs to anti-racist witch-hunters in the town hall. (The most dramatic case was that of the head teacher of a Brent school, Maureen McGoldrick, who was suspended for allegedly telling a council employee not to send her any more black teachers to fill vacant posts. Mrs McGoldrick's school had 80% black pupils taught by 75% white teachers). Conservative commentators spoke of a new Stalinism, challenged on the contradictory grounds of freedom of expression (on the one hand) and the need to challenge cultural relativism and promote national values (on the other).

But the left was critical too. Many argued that the often clumsy and ham-fisted character of much anti-racist practice was based on its politics. The 'prejudice-plus-power' definition of racism clearly implied that black people couldn't be racist – it also seemed to indicate that pretty much all white people were, and as a consequence so-called racism-awareness training often descended into provoking white guilt. One noted example of anti-racist ham-fistedness was the Burnage School in Manchester, where a thirteen-year-old boy called Ahmed Ullah was stabbed to death in September 1986. In his report on the case, Ian Macdonald QC criticised the school for failing to include white parents in discussions of its anti-racist policies (on the grounds that they were so irredeemably infected with racism that they could make no useful contribution) and for refusing to allow white children to attend Ahmed Ullah's funeral.

Left-wing critics saw anti-racism of this sort as individualised, failing to address the role of institutions and the state, and multiculturalism as depoliticised, recasting political oppression in cultural terms. They also noted that all the committees and grants, and the increasing number of black and Asian councillors and even MPs, were creating a new class which claimed to speak for communities with which it had less and less direct contact. As A. Sivanandan of the Institute of Race Relations put it, equal opportunities had mutated into equal opportunism. And both left and right criticised anti-racism for its rejection of and lack of interest in the white working class. For the right, the working class had born the brunt of the changes brought about by immigration. For the left, working-class people were being stigmatised for a racism which resulted from an imperial history whose crimes they had not committed and in whose benefits they hadn't shared.

As a result of all these criticisms, the harder edges of anti-racism were softened. Gradually, the word 'multiculturalism' gave way to the more inclusive 'diversity'. 'Prejudice-plus-power' was challenged by a new academic discipline called critical multiculturalism. Most of all, postmodern theory gave a theoretical foundation to what we observed all around us – a society of multiple identities, in which it was no longer possible to read a person's sexuality, habits or tastes off their ethnic group, in which (according to the last census) the second largest racial group in London is 'mixed'. The writings of Rushdie, Kureishi, Ishiguro expressed it, Robin Cook's 'Chicken Tikka Masala' speech celebrated it, the street life of North and West London, Birmingham and Manchester demonstrated it, and cultural theorist Paul Gilroy defined it as a new 'planetary humanism' in which the nation was 'a space of travelling cultures and peoples' with 'varying geographies of attachment'. As New Labour took power in 1997 on the basis of precisely this kind of vision, as a multi-identified, rainbow Britain was confirmed in the defining moment of Princess Diana's funeral, it appeared that a new consensus had indeed been established.

Even the institution most distrusted by Britain's non-white populations appeared to be catching up with the New Britain. The 1999 Macpherson report into the gross mishandling of the police investigation of the killing of Stephen Lawrence, a young black man stabbed to death by racists in East London, demonstrated that little had changed in police practice since Scarman. However, unlike Scarman, Sir William Macpherson blaimed these failings not on individual racist policemen, but what he called institutional racism, defined as 'the collective failure of an organisation to provide an appropriate and professional service to people because of their colour, culture or ethnic origin. It can be seen or detected in processes, attitudes and behaviour which amount to discrimination through unwitting prejudice, ignorance, thoughtlessness and racist stereotyping which disadvantage minority ethnic people'.

Macpherson was roundly attacked by the right-wing press, particularly for the institutional racism concept, which Leo McKinstry of *The Daily Telegraph* saw as the 'final triumph for town-hall political correctness'. For black and Asian community leaders, however, Macpherson expressed what they had been saying all along. Now, it was hoped and assumed, the police could combat its macho culture and its out-of-date procedures, and catch up with the multiply diverse Britain in which everyone else was happily living.

Well, not quite everybody. In 2001, Britain's newly worst-ever race riots broke out in three northern towns which were not so much multicultural as duocultural. Bradford, Oldham and Burnley had geographically concentrated Muslim communities of Pakistani/Bangladeshi origin which had felt threatened by far-right groups which held increasing sway over poor white working-class communities next door. In each case, attacks or the threat of attacks by neofascists triggered battles between the police and young Asian men seeking to defend their territories. Naturally, these three events spawned their own reports, all of which agreed that a major cause of the riots was divided communities (some spoke of parallel lives, others used the word 'apartheid'), which had been created partly by racist housing practices in the past, but which had now ossified into self-segregated enclaves with their own businesses, places of worship and – increasingly – schools. The post-riot reports identified other contributory factors: first, a group of self-appointed ethnic leaders, sustained by public grant-aid, and failing to speak for their communities; second, defence of illiberal cultural practices like forced marriages, oppression of women and homophobia, on the grounds of religious tradition; third, ineffective policing of the increasing drugs trade involving young Asian men; and fourth, resentment in poor white working-class areas of perceived privileges for slightly-poorer Asian areas. In other words, many of the accusations against the anti-racism of the 1980s, from right and left, were coming home to roost. The 2001 riots appeared to be the unintended consequences of well-meaning policies that had dominated the preceding twenty years.

The result of this was a change of course, summed up in the policy of community cohesion. The North of England area Commission for Racial Equality spoke bleakly about self-segregation that would take decades to correct. ('We may have already arrived at a degree of segregation which would not be reversible over, say, a decade, without serious social dislocation.') Home Secretary David Blunkett criticised the failure of some South-Asian families to learn English, and instituted an oath of loyalty to be spoken by all new citizens, not only declaring 'true allegiance to Her Majesty, Queen Elizabeth the Second, her Heirs and Successors according to law', but also pledging to respect Britain's 'rights and freedoms', to uphold its 'democratic values' and to observe its laws. The national report on the 2001 riots, written by Ted Cantle, stated that 'a meaningful concept of "citizenship" needs establishing – and championing – which recognises (in education programmes in particular) the contribution of all cultures to this Nation's development throughout its history, but establishes a clear primary loyalty to this Nation'.

The debate about community cohesion spilled over into a more general debate about multiculturalism. In February 2004, David Goodhart, editor of the left-leaning journal *Prospect*, wrote a long article arguing that there was a contradiction between the welfare state and diversity, in that the welfare state relied on people being prepared to pay taxes to help other people, which they're only prepared to do if the people they're helping are like themselves. (He concluded that where principles of community and diversity collide, the principles of community should take precedence, arguing for traditional British history to be taught in schools and suggesting that temporary workers should have limited legal rights, and that a two-tier welfare system might be imposed.) Attacking Goodhart for racism, Commission for Racial Equality head Trevor Phillips none-theless declared (in April) that multiculturalism was out of date, as it encouraged separateness, for which he was praised by *Guardian* columnist Polly Toynbee for breaking 'with unctuous, unthinking platitudes about the richness of all diversity in a multicultural society, as if any difference was a self-evident asset'. Toynbee went on to connect the flight from multiculturalism with 9/11: 'We are looking into the face of an insane and unassuagable cult. No kind of multiculturalism "understands" this.'

At the same time, the British National Party cemented its electoral gains, in the wake of the riots, in Lancashire, Yorkshire and the Midlands. Despite what was for them a disappointing performance in the 2004 local elections, the BNP gained over 800,000 votes in the European elections. They would have got more had some of their support not gone to the right-wing populist UK Independence Party, who won two and a half million votes on a manifesto claiming that Britain is 'full up'. And in the 2005 General Election, the BNP polled nearly 200,000 votes, winning 16.9% of the vote in Barking, 13.1% in Dewsbury and 10.3% in Burnley.

The move away from multiculturalism is part of a more general, post-9/11 European trend. In a recent edition of the journal *Race and Class*, France's Social Affairs Minister is quoted as criticising 'communautarisme' for creating a 'guilty mentality which has led our country to doubt its own values and its own history'. The Dutch Prime Minister insists that Holland 'does not constitute an aggregation of different cultures', while the former Spanish Prime Minister claims that multiculturalism splits society. As a result, these and other countries have introduced 'integration contracts', of which the most extensive is the Dutch (where the Immigration and Integration Minister directed imams to preach in the Dutch language). Europe-wide, there is an attack on dual nationality. French planners deny permission for mosques with domes or minarets, Rotterdam turned down plans for a new mosque considered 'too Arabic' and two German states ban teachers from wearing headscarves as an expression of a 'lack of cultural integration'. More recently, France, Germany and Spain introduced legislation to make it easier to deport what the German legislation calls 'intellectual incendiaries'. Following the November 2004 murder of Dutch filmmaker Theo van Gogh (whose film *Submission* included shots of naked female bodies decorated with verses from the Koran), residence rights were removed from three imams who had tolerated the recruitment of Muslims for jihad and urged Muslims 'to isolate themselves from Dutch society'.

In Britain, the failures of multiculturalism were identified as a key contributor to the 2005 London bombings. Three weeks after 7th July, the BBC's 'Today' programme went back to the 2001 riot reports (particularly Cantle), citing their criticism of self-segregated Muslim communities, and drawing a line between the events of 2001 and 2005. In addition to renewed attacks on multiculturalism from people who had always opposed it (like *Prospect*'s David Goodhart), liberal journalists and journals raised uncomfortable questions. While remaining hostile to French assimilationism, *The Guardian*'s 1 August leader shared Ted Cantle's fears about polarised communities. The day before, *The Observer* declared that Britain had 'tilted too far towards multiculturalism', that it 'should not aim to be an umbrella nation sheltering a range of separate ethnic and religious groups but a single nation with far more of a single identity'. Calling for compulsory English lessons for new arrivals and condemning the wearing of the veil in schools, the newspaper declared that 'core British values should be part of everybody's lives'.

So, is Roy Jenkins' vision of a society of mutual tolerance and respect now fracturing into isolated communities of difference, glowering at each other across self-imposed ethnic and cultural divides? There are three possible answers.

One view – probably the dominant one before 7th July 2005 – is that this fracturing exists, but it doesn't exist everywhere. In Britain, the future doesn't lie in the mosques and pubs of the declining mill towns of East Lancs and West Yorks but in the coffee shops and late-night foodstores and fusion restaurants and indeed discotheques of the big metropolitan centres, where the world sits with its latte and its laptop, contemplating where it's going to go today. In this view – and despite the shock of the 7th July – we have seen the future, it's postmodern and it works.

The second answer is informed by recent events. Duoculture may be exceptional but it's important, because it is the breeding ground for terrorism. And while it may be at its most extreme and visible in places like Burnley, Bradford and Oldham, it's now clear that segregated enclaves exist in the forgotten crevices of Latteland as well. Reliant on a single, now-dead industry, the mill towns are the most extreme expression of the social exclusion that results from globalisation. But, like rocks standing proud of the sea at high tide, they may reveal an underlying geology.

What the current debate is not addressing is a necessary corollary to both these perspectives: the idea that a successfully plural multiculturalism is a two-way street. However petrified it may have become, the segregation of the northern towns is a legacy of discriminatory policies in the past (in 1990 and 1993, the Commission for Racial Equality found policies of discrimination still existed in both private and public housing in Oldham). The difference between Oldham and Leicester, Burnley and Birmingham and indeed Bradford and London is not the concentration of populations but relative wealth. If multiculturalism is to fulfill its promise as a conversation between cultures, then the majority culture has to listen to Islam's emphasis on social compassion, as Islam should listen to the host culture's (relatively recent) commitment to sexual tolerance.

Most important, if we are not to return to 1950s notions of national loyalty (and the national history), then attention needs to be paid to the forging of a collective identity applicable to the present day. Most people agree that the things which will bind us together are going to be principles: democracy, the rule of law, welfare, respect for minority rights but respect too for minorities within those minorities. But we live in a time when the institutions which can define and deliver those principles are atrophied. The popular newspapers, television news, local government, the political parties, the trade unions and churches are all less predominant, less confident and less competent than they were twenty years ago. Before we criticise the 'multi' bit of multiculturalism we need to look to health of the culture bit, which is currently woeful, and dangerously so.

If the mechanisms to promote, develop and deepen those principles from above are rusty, then it is hard to detect the wellsprings of hope bubbling up from below. Nonetheless, there are efforts in the hardest places to challenge community division, not through integrating residence, which will take years, nor by integrating schooling, which follows residence, not even through the workplace, which following the decline of trade unionism is no longer the site of communication and development that it was twenty years ago, even where the workplace still exists as such at all. It is happening through culture. And everyone working in this field agrees that the thing you don't do, when attempting to get groups of young people to know more about each other, is to bring one side into the other's territory. Rather, you create third spaces, unfamiliar to both, in which different groups can share a similar experience of discovery. Sometimes such spaces allow people to detach aspects of their identity (cultural, vocational, sexual) from what they have hitherto regarded as its essential and dominating character. Often, it is within rather than between groups that the real processes of discovery occur. In any event, it is in such spaces – youth groups, drama workshops, sports teams – that some of the most imaginative and successful forms of community healing have taken place.

DAVID EDGAR
August 2005